BOSTON

ENCOUNTER

MARA V

Boston Encounter

Published by Lonely Planet Publications Pty Ltd
ABN 36 005 607 983

Australia	Head Office, Locked Bag 1, Footscray, Vic 3011
	☎ 03 8379 8000 fax 03 8379 8111
	talk2us@lonelyplanet.com.au
USA	150 Linden St, Oakland, CA 94607
	☎ 510 250 6400
	toll free 800 275 8555
	fax 510 893 8572
	info@lonelyplanet.com
UK	2nd fl, 186 City Rd
	London EC1V 2NT
	☎ 020 7106 2100 fax 020 7106 2101
	go@lonelyplanet.co.uk

This title was commissioned in Lonely Planet's Oakland office and produced by: **Commissioning Editor** Jennye Garibaldi **Coordinating Editor** Averil Robertson **Coordinating Cartographer** David Kemp **Coordinating Layout Designer** Frank Deim **Assisting Editors** Michelle Bennett, Kirsten Rawlings **Assisting Cartographer** Marc Milinkovic **Assisting Layout Designer** Pablo Gastar **Managing Editors** Imogen Bannister, Geoff Howard **Managing Cartographer** David Connolly **Cover** Image Research provided by lonelyplanetimages.com **Project Manager** Rachel Imeson **Managing Layout Designer** Laura Jane **Thanks to** David Burnett, Amanda Canning, Sally Darmody, Huw Fowles, Michelle Glynn, Wayne Murphy

ISBN 978 1 74179 603 2

Printed through Colorcraft Ltd, Hong Kong. Printed in China.

Acknowledgement © 2008 Massachusetts Bay Transportation Authority

HOW TO USE THIS BOOK
Color-Coding & Maps
Color-coding is used for symbols on maps and in the text that they relate to (eg all eating venues on the maps and in the text are given a green knife and fork symbol). Each neighborhood also gets its own color, and this is used down the edge of the page and throughout that neighborhood section.

Prices
Multiple prices listed with reviews (eg $10/5 or $10/5/20) indicate adult/child, adult/concession or adult/child/family.

MARA VORHEES

Born and raised in St Clair Shores, Michigan, Mara traveled the world before finally settling in the Hub. She now lives in a pink house in Somerville, Massachusetts. She spent several years pushing papers and tapping keys at Harvard University, but has since embraced the life of a full-time travel writer, traveling to destinations as diverse as Russia and Belize. When in Boston, she is often spotted sipping Sam Seasonal in Union Sq and pedaling her road bike along the Charles River. Mara is the coauthor of Lonely Planet's *New England* and the *Boston City Guide*. She has also written for *National Geographic Traveler* and *Boston Globe* Travel. Follow her adventures online at www.maravorhees.com.

MARA'S THANKS

To my Local Voices – Barbara Lynch, John Jacobs, Thomas O'Connor, Adam Roffman and Jimmy Tingle – for sharing suggestions and posing for pics. To my patient editor, Jennye Garibaldi, for giving me an assignment close to home. To my patient husband, for sharing his city with me.

THE PHOTOGRAPHER

Lou Jones specializes in location photography for corporate and editorial clients including Federal Express, Nike, National Geographic and Aetna. He has completed assignments in 46 countries, photographing royalty and the third world, the sacred and profane. With a lifelong passion for photojournalism and social documentary, Jones has worked with institutions such as Amnesty International, and has photographed many jazz legends, including Miles Davis, 12 Olympic Games, and inmates on death row. Jones's work is included in collections at Smithsonian Institution, DeCordova Museum, Gallery Saintonge, and the Center for Fine Art Photography.

Cover photograph Boat sails under a bridge on the Charles River with the buildings of downtown Boston in the background, Kevin Fleming/Corbis. **Internal photographs** p142 Brandon Presser; p10 Sharon/Alamy; p4 Stock Connection Distribution/Alamy. All other photographs by Lonely Planet Images, and by Lou Jones except Brian Cruickshank p69; Richard Cummins p15, p32 (top right); Lee Foster p21; p31; Kim Grant p8, p12, p17, p22, p24, p27, p29, p32 (bottom), p36, p43, p59, p60, p80, p135, p137, p138, p146, p149, p151; Hanan Isachar p123; Gareth McCormack p6 (top); Angus Oborn p104, p140.

All images are copyright of the photographers unless otherwise indicated. Many of the images in this guide are available for licensing from **Lonely Planet Images:** www.lonelyplanetimages.com

Cheer on the Boston Red Sox (p112) like a local

CONTENTS

Why is our travel information the best in the world? It's simple: our authors are passionate, dedicated travelers. They don't take freebies in exchange for positive coverage so you can be sure the advice you're given is impartial. They travel widely to all the popular spots, and off the beaten track. They don't research using just the internet or phone. They discover new places not included in any other guidebook. They personally visit thousands of hotels, restaurants, palaces, trails, galleries, temples and more. They speak with dozens of locals every day to make sure you get the kind of insider knowledge only a local could tell you. They take pride in getting all the details right, and in telling it how it is. Think you can do it? Find out how at **lonelyplanet.com**.

THIS IS BOSTON

Exiting Kendall Square, the red-line train emerges from the tunnel into the daylight. It trundles over the Longfellow Bridge, offering up 360 degrees of river, sky and city.

The sun glints off the River Charles, framing the sailboats that float silently in the basin. The handsome Back Bay brownstones line up along the shore in an orderly fashion, while the backdrop is a haphazard assembly of skyscraper spires. In the east, the gold dome of the State House peaks out from its perch on Beacon Hill. And in the west shines the Citgo sign. The passengers on the T take a momentary break from their commute to marvel at their city.

If Boston is lovely to look at from afar, she is even more intriguing up close. These narrow streets recall a history of revolution and transformation: Puritans fleeing persecution and setting up their model society; patriots protesting tyranny and building a new nation; philosophers and poets preaching and penning to change their world for the better.

Today, Boston is still among the country's forward-thinking and barrier-breaking cities. This is most evident politically, where it is at the forefront of controversial issues such as supporting same-sex marriage and universal healthcare. It's also visible in the changing landscape of the city; Boston and its environs are now home to some of the country's most cutting-edge architecture and innovative urban-planning projects. Culturally, Boston is shedding its staid and stodgy reputation, with a flourishing contemporary art and film scene.

No single element has influenced the city so profoundly as its educational institutions. As in the past, Boston's universities and colleges continue to attract scholars, scientists, philosophers and writers who shape the city's evolving culture. Students arrive from around the world, an endless source of energy for the youthful city.

Now the train has pulled into Park St station. Elbows out. Eyes alert. Let's see what Boston is all about.

Top Bustling Long Wharf on Boston's waterfront **Bottom** A wintry day on Commonwealth Ave in Back Bay)

>HIGHLIGHTS

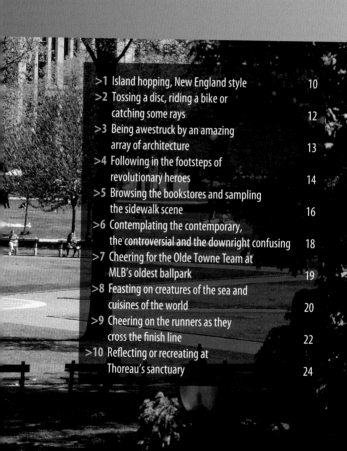

The Boston Common sits at the heart of the city (p58)

>1 BOSTON HARBOR ISLANDS
ISLAND HOPPING, NEW ENGLAND STYLE

It used to be easy to forget that Boston is a coastal city. For so many years, the waterfront was an unsavory, unsatisfying urban stretch. It was hard to get to, cut off by the traffic-laden Central Artery and later the Big Dig construction zone. More importantly, it was pointless to get to. Who wants to hang out amidst abandoned warehouses and polluted waters?

Times have changed, all ye seafaring folk. Following a massive, multimillion-dollar cleanup in the mid-1990s, the Boston Harbor now provides a spectacular scenic backdrop to the city, and its 34 islands provide an exciting urban-adventure destination for day-trippers and city-scapers.

If you are sailing your own boat, your options are unlimited. The islands are your oyster. Otherwise, it's easy to get out to Georges Island or Spectacle Island by taking the Harbor Express ferry from Long Wharf. Either of these can serve as a launching pad to visiting the other islands – and they are also destinations in their own right.

Georges Island is the site of Fort Warren, a 19th-century fort and Civil War prison which is largely abandoned, with many dark tunnels, creepy corners and magnificent lookouts to discover. Spectacle Island is a bit more civilized. After a recent revamp, it has a brand new marina, supervised beaches and a solar-powered visitors center. Five miles of walking trails provide access to a 157ft peak overlooking the harbor.

Other islands offer other adventures. Catch the interisland shuttle to Lovells Island to lounge on the rocky beach and to run with the rabbits; or to Grape Island to hunt for wild raspberries, bayberries and elderberries. Explore the remains of Fort Andrews on Peddocks Island, or follow the trails through fields of wildflowers on Bumpkin Island.

True salty dogs can take a tour out to Little Brewster to investigate the iconic Boston Light, the oldest light station, which dates to 1715. Climb the 76 steps to the top of the light for a close-up view of the rotating light and a far-off view of the city skyline.

And if that's not ample reminder that Boston is a city on the sea... see p68 for more.

>2 CHARLES RIVER ESPLANADE

TOSSING A DISC, RIDING A BIKE OR CATCHING SOME RAYS

We can thank Frederick Law Olmsted for transforming the marshy, mucky Charles River Basin into Boston's favorite urban greenscape. In typical Olmsted style, the Esplanade is a centerpiece of the city, accessible from Beacon Hill, the Back Bay and further west in Brighton. It is an enticing and easy escape from the city, a delightful oasis that is always abuzz with hikers and bikers, runners and sunners, picnickers and play-scapers.

Free concerts and movies at the Hatch Memorial Shell are highlights of summer in the city. Indeed, this is where Boston's Independence Day celebration goes down, with a week of festivities leading up to the Boston Pops playing the 1812 Overture and an amazing display of fireworks lighting up the city sky.

See p99 for more information.

>3 COPLEY SQUARE

BEING AWESTRUCK BY AN AMAZING ARRAY OF ARCHITECTURE

Step onto Copley Sq and into the 'Athens of America.' Boston's most magnificent architecture is clustered around this Back Bay plaza, symbolic of the culture and learning that gave Boston its nickname in the 19th century.

Facing off across the square are two masterpieces, each representing a pinnacle of artistic design. On one side, the original McKim building, which houses the Boston Public Library (p92), was inspired by an Italian Renaissance palazzo. Through Daniel Chester French's bronze doorways, the library is filled with amazing murals (not to mention books).

At the opposite end of the square, the crowning achievement of Henry Hobson Richardson is the elaborate Romanesque Trinity Church (p93), its interior adorned with magnificent stained glass.

And here – off in the corner – stands Boston's tallest, shiniest skyscraper, the John Hancock Tower, designed by James Cobb. But instead of stealing the show, it gracefully reflects the gorgeousness of the church in its mirrored glass façade.

>4 FREEDOM TRAIL

FOLLOWING IN THE FOOTSTEPS OF REVOLUTIONARY HEROES

Summon your inner Paul Revere and follow the red-brick road, from the Boston Common to the Bunker Hill Monument, past 16 sites where the most dramatic scenes from history played out.

This walking trail is the best introduction to revolutionary Boston, tracing the locations of the events that earned this town its status as the cradle of liberty. The 2.5-mile trail follows the course of the conflict, from the Old State House (p70), where the Redcoats killed five men, to the Old North Church (p48), where the sexton hung two lanterns to warn of the British advance. Along the way, it passes Faneuil Hall (p68), the old market and meeting place, and the Old South Meeting House (p69), where protesters planned the Boston Tea Party.

Even though it's called the Freedom Trail, it covers much more than just revolutionary history. Here you'll find some of Boston's oldest landmarks, including three cemeteries dating to the 17th century, America's first public park and the site of its first public school. You'll also find the sites where Boston prospered in the postrevolutionary period – the Massachusetts State House (p58), built for the new Commonwealth in 1798; Park St Church (p59), where abolitionists rallied in 1829; the Old Corner Bookstore, where literary salons were held

FREEDOM FACTS

> Great elm or gallows? The Boston Common was a popular spot for hanging religious heretics during Puritan times (p58).
> A statue of a hooker in front of the State House? That would be the Civil War General 'Fighting Joe' Hooker (p58).
> Paul Revere was not the only midnight rider. Pay your respects at the Granary Burying Ground (p58), but don't neglect William Dawes, buried at King's Chapel (p68), and Samuel Prescott, buried in Concord (p125).
> Whose hill? Turns out the Battle of Bunker Hill took place on Breed's Hill, which is where the monument stands today (p42).

throughout the 19th century; and the Charlestown Navy Yard (p42), active into the 20th century.

This well-trafficked walking tour is officially operated by the National Park Service (NPS; p168). It starts on the Boston Common, passes through Beacon Hill, Downtown and the North End, before crossing the bridge and ending in Charlestown. As such, the Freedom Trail provides an introduction to some of Boston's distinct neighborhoods and its rich history.

>5 HARVARD SQUARE

BROWSING THE BOOKSTORES AND SAMPLING THE SIDEWALK SCENE

Although many Cantabrigians rightly complain that the square has lost its edge – shops once independently owned are continually being gobbled up by national chains – Harvard Sq is still a vibrant, exciting place to hang out.

There's a lot to Harvard Sq besides the university: it's a hotbed of colonial and revolutionary history. Opposite the main entrance to Harvard Yard is Cambridge Common, the village green where General Washington took command of the Continental Army on July 3, 1775. The traffic island at the south end, known as Dawes Island, pays tribute to the 'other rider' William Dawes, who rode through here on April 18, 1775, to warn that the British were coming (look for bronze hoofprints embedded in the sidewalk). From here you can stroll over to Brattle St, the epitome of colonial posh. Lined with mansions that were once home to royal sympathizers, it earned the nickname Tory Row. But its proximity to the university also means that it is a well-known address for the country's intellectual elite.

There are no official stats, but Harvard Sq must have one of the country's richest selections of bookstores. (Again, old-timers complain that there are not as many as there used to be, but there are still a lot.) The listings on p117 just begin to scratch the surface. Explore the back streets and alleyways and you'll find used bookstores, new bookstores, poetry bookstores, academic bookstores, children's bookstores, travel bookstores, foreign-language bookstores and more.

UNOFFICIAL TOUR

This unofficial Harvard tour (☎ 203-305-9735; www.harv.unofficialtours.com; donations accepted) was founded by two dynamic alums, 'a New England liberal and a conservative Texan.' The idea is to allow students to give the inside scoop on Harvard's history and life at 'The University'. Tours depart at least twice daily from the Cambridge Visitor Information Kiosk outside the Harvard Sq T station. Check the website for the current schedule.

Once you have your reading material, take a seat at one of Harvard Sq's many sidewalk cafés. From here you have a front-row view of the congregations of students, the performances of buskers, the bustle of the shoppers, the pleas of the homeless and the challenges between chess players.

See p114 for more information.

>6 INSTITUTE FOR CONTEMPORARY ART

CONTEMPLATING THE CONTEMPORARY, THE CONTROVERSIAL AND THE DOWNRIGHT CONFUSING

Boston may appear radical in its politics, but in affairs of the art, the city has long shown more conservative tastes. The 2006 unveiling of a gleaming new Institute of Contemporary Art (ICA) on the waterfront shattered this trend, establishing the city as a hub for the art of the present and the future.

A growing appreciation for art after Arles led to the construction of the city's first major art building in over 100 years. Like most contemporary art museums, the ICA is as much about the space as it is about the art. The four-story cantilevered gallery on Fan Pier appears to hover over the harbor. Its tall glass walls eliminate the boundary between the interior and exterior. The space allows for art in all its forms, including multimedia presentations, educational programs and studio space.

Contemporary art attempts to be about real social issues and uses real materials from everyday life as a means of expression; in this way, the design of the building already fulfills the mission of the ICA, 'to become both a dynamic space for public activity and a contemplative space for experiencing the art of our time.'

See p78 for more information.

>7 FENWAY PARK

CHEERING FOR THE OLDE TOWNE TEAM AT MLB'S OLDEST BALLPARK

The oldest of the old-style baseball parks has been home to the Boston Red Sox since 1912 – that's almost a century of baseball.

Fans will never forget that the Sox went without a championship for 86 of those years. They came so close to winning so many times that there had to be some supernatural explanation. Woe is the Fenway Faithful, it was long said, for their team is cursed.

Whether the spiteful spirit of Babe Ruth really held sway at Fenway Park, nobody knows. But something happened in 2004 to change the team's history of defeat, and the Boston Red Sox became World Series Champs. Proof that the curse really was reversed came with a repeat victory in 2007.

And that only enhances the unique thrill of watching baseball at Fenway Park. Only at Fenway do long fly balls get lost in the Triangle, the furthest corner of center field. Only Fenway has the Green Monster, the towering left-field wall that constantly alters the play of the game. And only at Fenway do fans sing along with Neil Diamond as he croons 'Sweet Caroline' at the bottom of the eighth inning.

Now, with the Sox consistently playing at the top of their division, the Fenway Faithful are in fine form. 'Good times never seemed so good.'

See p112 for more information.

>8 NORTH END TO SOUTH END

FEASTING ON CREATURES OF THE SEA AND CUISINES OF THE WORLD

Boston is the home of the first Thanksgiving and of bountiful autumnal harvests. It is America's seafood capital, famed for clam chowder and boiled lobster. And it is a rich mix of ethnic flavors from all corners of the world. Is your mouth watering yet?

Anyone who wishes to eat their way across Boston will surely start in the North End (p50), the city's most storied food quarter. A tight-knit immigrant enclave, the North End became an exemplar for old-fashioned Italian-American cooking, with tomato sauces simmering and pasta boiling on every stove. It still smells like the Old World, with aromas of garlic and oregano emanating from every window.

In this era of creative culinary discovery, Bostonians are reclaiming their roots in one crucial way: their appreciation of fresh, seasonal and organic products. And nowhere is this trend more apparent than at Haymarket (p72), the colorful, chaotic produce market that takes place on Fridays and Saturdays. Here you will find the cheapest produce in town, and everybody and their brother haggling over it.

Once you escape the market, you can nibble your way across Downtown (p71), sampling the falafels, burritos, hot dogs and ginormous sandwiches that provide the fuel for this workaday world.

A diversion across the Fort Point Channel into the Seaport District lands you in seafood central. Now *this* is what you came to Boston for. Go for the classic fish sandwich or an irresistible lobster roll from one of the restaurants or retail outlets that line the fish piers (p80).

Your next stop is Chinatown (p84), a few small square blocks that are crammed with flavors and textures. And they are surprisingly diverse, ranging from Chinese dumplings to Vietnamese *pho* to pad thai to Japanese sushi to Korean *bi bim bop*. It's a culinary microcosm of Asia that could keep you fed for years.

Finally you find yourself in the South End (p103). This is Boston's trendiest, foodiest neighborhood. Here, all the earlier elements come together – the fresh seafood, the seasonal produce, the ethnic influences – in an explosion of eclectic, creative cooking.

>9 BOSTON MARATHON
CHEERING ON THE RUNNERS AS THEY CROSS THE FINISH LINE

Patriots' Day – officially celebrated on the third Monday in April – means more than Paul Revere's ride and 'the shot heard around the world.' Since 1897, Patriots' Day has also meant the Boston Marathon. Fifteen people ran that first race (only 10 finished); these days, the Boston Marathon attracts over 20,000 participants annually.

The 26-mile race starts in rural Hopkinton, Massachusetts, and winds its way through the western suburbs of Ashland, Natick, Wellesley, Newton and Brookline to Boston. Some of the marathon's most dramatic moments occur between mile 20 and mile 21, where the course runs through the notorious Newton Hills. On Commonwealth Ave, near Boston College, it culminates at the aptly named Heartbreak Hill, rising a steep 80ft. It's all downhill from there.

Runners cruise up Beacon St, through Kenmore Sq, down Commonwealth Ave, turning right on Hereford St and left on Boylston St, and into a triumphant finish at Copley Sq. This final mile is among the most exciting places spectators can base themselves.

Women began running in the Boston Marathon only in the 1960s. Roberta Gibb was the first woman to run in 1966, but she ran without properly registering, hiding in the bushes until the start of the race. The following year, Katherine Switzer entered as 'KV Switzer.' When race officials realized a female was in the Boston Marathon, they tried to physically remove her from the course. The rules were changed in 1971, and the following year eight women ran the Marathon.

The most infamous participant (loosely defined) is probably Rosie Ruiz, who in 1980 seemingly emerged from nowhere to win the women's division. In fact, it was determined that she did emerge from nowhere and had skipped most of the race. She was disqualified, but remains a marathon legend.

Other marathon celebrities include Rick and Dick Hoyt (www.team hoyt.com), a famous father-son team. Rick has cerebral palsy, due to severe brain damage at birth. Father Dick is determined to give his son the chance to pursue his passions, including sports. With Dick pushing his son in a wheelchair and using other special equipment, they have competed in 66 marathons and over 200 triathlons. The Hoyts have completed the Boston Marathon 26 times. Are you inspired yet?

See p27 for more information.

>10 WALDEN POND

REFLECTING OR RECREATING AT THOREAU'S SANCTUARY

'I went to the woods because I wished to live deliberately, to front only the essential facts of life, and see if I could not learn what it had to teach, and not, when I came to die, discover that I had not lived.' So wrote Henry David Thoreau about his time at Walden Pond. Thoreau took the naturalist beliefs of transcendentalism out of the realm of theory and into practice when he left the comforts of Concord and built himself a rustic cabin on the shores of the pond. His famous memoir of his time spent there, *Walden, or Life in the Woods* (1854), was full of praise for nature and disapproval of the stresses of civilized life -- sentiments that have found an eager audience ever since.

The glacial pond is now a state park, surrounded by acres of forest preserved by the Walden Woods project, a nonprofit organization. The site of Thoreau's cabin is on the northeast side of the pond, marked by a cairn and signs.

Although there's a swimming beach and facilities on the southern side, you're better off following the footpath that circles the pond to escape the crowds and find a private place on the deserted northern end. Certainly that's what Thoreau would have done.

See p125 for more information.

>BOSTON CALENDAR

Boston's calendar is packed with events to suit all sorts of revelers, from sports fans to culture vultures, from music mavens to food freaks, from history buffs to buff historians. (Well, maybe there is not a special event for scholars with muscles, but they certainly won't be excluded from participating in the revolutionary reenactments!) Boston's diverse population guarantees an intriguing — even exotic — array of international events from Chinese New Year to Italian religious festivals, and few cities can rival its rich calendar of cultural events. For comprehensive information see http://calendar.boston.com or www.bostonusa.com.

The infamous Boston Tea Party is reenacted in December (p30)

JANUARY

Martin Luther King Day

www.mlkday.gov

The third Monday in January is a day of service, when everybody is encouraged to remember Rev Martin Luther King by doing something positive for the community. Take advantage of the many one-day volunteer opportunities at schools, hospitals, shelters, soup kitchens and community organizations around the city.

FEBRUARY

Chinese New Year

www.chinatownmainstreet.org

In late January or early February, Chinatown lights up with a colorful parade, firecrackers, fireworks and lots of food. Highlights of the celebration include eating *xiaolongbao* (soupy dumplings) and watching the star performance by the Dragon & Lion Dance Troupe.

MARCH

St Patrick's Day

www.saintpatricksdayparade.com/boston

Ireland's patron saint is honored on March 17 by those who feel the Irish in their blood and those who want to feel Irish beer in their blood.

Restaurant Week

www.restaurantweekboston.com

Two weeks, really: one in March and one at the end of August. Participating restaurants around the city offer prix-fixe menus: lunch $20, dinner $30.

The Boston Irish love the St Patrick's Day celebration, to be sure

APRIL

Patriots' Day

www.battleroad.org

Held on the third Monday, Patriots' Day commemorates the start of the American Revolution, with reenactments in Lexington and Concord.

Boston Marathon

☎ 617-236-1652; www.boston marathon.org

Thousands compete in this 26.2-mile race – the longest-running marathon in the world. Held on Patriots' Day.

Independent Film Festival of Boston

www.iffboston.org

Innovative shorts, documentaries and dramatic films are screened around the city during the final week of April.

Modern-day patriots on Patriots' Day

when more than 400 varieties of fragrant lilac are in bloom.

MAY

MayFair

www.harvardsquare.com

When the sun comes out, so do the good folks in Harvard Sq. This street fair, featuring artists, merchants, musicians and children's events, is held on the first Sunday of May.

Lilac Sunday

www.arboretum.harvard.edu

On the third Sunday of May, Arnold Arboretum celebrates the arrival of spring,

JUNE

Boston Pride Festival

☎ 617-262-9405; www.bostonpride.org

The Pride Parade, a highlight of the festival, attracts thousands of participants decked out in outrageous costumes. Held in the first week of June.

Bunker Hill Day

Charlestown reenacts the Battle of Bunker Hill, followed by a parade and road race, on June 17.

The North End bands together in August for feasts and processions honoring their patron saints

Life Is Good Festival

www.lifeisgood.com

The local company with the optimistic outlook sponsors music and fun on the Boston Common on the third weekend of June.

JULY

Harborfest

☎ 617-227-1528; www.boston
harborfest.com

In the first week of July, festivities including Children's Day (play kids' games) and Chowderfest (eat fish soup) lead up to Independence Day.

Independence Day

www.july4th.org

Boston hosts a lineup of free performances on the Esplanade on July 4, culminating with the Boston Pops playing Tchaikovsky's 1812 Overture, complete with synchronized fireworks.

AUGUST

Boston Carnival

www.bostoncarnival.org

A real Caribbean Carnival, complete with spectacular costumes, sultry music and spicy cooking. Includes the Kiddies Carnival Celebration and the all-out, over-the-top 'Trini-style' parade. Held in the third week of August.

Italian Festivals

www.northendboston.com
/news-religious.htm

The North End's religious societies sponsor feasts and processions over the last two weekends of August, honoring their patron saints. Major celebrations include the Fisherman's Feast and St Anthony's Feast.

SEPTEMBER

River Sing
www.revels.org

Revelers line the banks of the Charles River to celebrate the first day of fall with song.

Blues Trust
www.bluestrust.com

Got the blues? Enjoy two days of (free) blues music at the Hatch Memorial Shell on the last weekend of September.

Head of the Charles Regatta

Berklee Beantown Jazz Festival
☎ 617-747-2260; www.beantown jazz.com

Berklee sponsors two days of free music, panel discussions, kids' activities and all that jazz. Last weekend of September.

OCTOBER

Oktoberfest
www.harvardsquare.com

Harvard Sq artisans and entertainers take to the streets on the first Sunday of the month to entertain children with puppet shows, face painting, fair rides and dance troupes.

Head of the Charles Regatta
☎ 617-868-6200; www.hocr.org

The Charles River hosts the world's largest rowing event on the third weekend of October, drawing thousands of collegiate, club and independent rowers. Fans line the riverbanks.

Pumpkin Festival
www.campsunshine.org

Good deed–doers and good gourd-carvers descend on City Hall Plaza to carve pumpkins for a cause. Boston currently holds the record for the most lit jack-o'-lanterns.

Haunted Happenings
www.hauntedhappenings.org

Salem celebrates Halloween for the entire month, culminating on October 31, with the crowning of the King and Queen of Halloween. Oooh, that's scary.

OTHER ARTISTIC EVENTS

Artistic events occur throughout the year, even in unexpected places. This is the Athens of America, after all.

> **Film Festivals at the MFA** Throughout the year, the Museum of Fine Arts (p110) hosts film festivals dedicated to every culture on the planet (Jewish, Iranian, African, French etc) as well as a gay and lesbian film festival and the Human Rights Watch film festival.

> **First Fridays** The SoWa Artists Guild (Map p101; www.sowaartistsguild.com; 450 Harrison Ave; ⏱ 5-9pm first Fri) hosts an open-studios event on the first Friday of every month.

> **Hatch Shell Friday Flicks & Free Concerts** (www.hatchshell.com) In summer, local radio stations sponsor free movies (Friday nights, mid-June to August) and free concerts on the Charles River Esplanade.

> **Shakespeare on the Common** Hosted by the Citi Performing Arts Center. A summer stage on the Boston Common shows free Shakespeare to crowds of picnickers and theater-lovers.

NOVEMBER

America's Hometown Thanksgiving Celebration

www.usathanksgiving.com

Historic Plymouth comes to life on the weekend before Thanksgiving as Pilgrims, pioneers and patriots parade the streets of 'America's Hometown.' The weekend event features a food festival, a concert series, a craft show and the ongoing festivities at the 'historic village.'

DECEMBER

Boston Tea Party Reenactment

www.oldsouthmeetinghouse.org

Costumed actors march from Old South Meeting House to the waterfront and toss crates of tea into the harbor on the Sunday before December 16.

First Night

www.firstnight.org

New Year celebrations begin early on December 31 and continue past midnight, culminating in fireworks over the harbor. A special button permits entrance into events citywide.

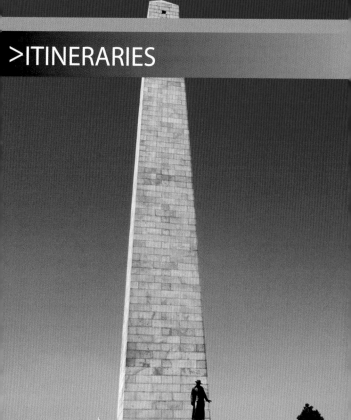

Climb 295 steps up to the Bunker Hill Monument (p42)

ITINERARIES

So much fun, so little time. With Boston's abundance of dramatic history, cool campuses, picture-perfect parks, marvelous museums, classy culture and excellent eating, you'll want to experience as much as possible. Make every day count by following these suggestions for ways to spend your days in Boston.

DAY ONE

The Freedom Trail is the perfect one-day introduction to Boston. You'll hit the city's most historically significant sights, and you won't even need a map. Just follow the red-brick road that leads from the Boston Common (p58) through Downtown Boston to the North End and across the bridge to Charlestown. Along the way you can snag a sandwich at Chacarero (p74) or enjoy a leisurely lunch at Legal Sea Foods (p73). After climbing to the top of the Bunker Hill Monument (p42), the final Freedom Trail stop, you may want to recharge at Zumes Coffee House (p45). But save room for dinner... an Italian feast at Giacomo's Ristorante (p51) or Pomodoro (p52) in the North End.

DAY TWO

For a day of window shopping and gallery hopping, stroll down Newbury St. Investigate the art on exhibit at Barbara Krakow Gallery (p92) and NAGA Gallery (p92) and shop for souvenirs at boutiques such as Oak (p95) and Jake's House (p94). For lunch stop at Parish Café & Bar (p97) for a gourmet sandwich invented by one of Boston's celebrity chefs. Then head to Copley Sq to gawk at the stunning assemblage of buildings, including Trinity Church (p93) and the Boston Public Library (p92). See the spot where Boston Marathon runners cross the finish line, and if you're really inspired head to Marathon Sports (p95) to buy some new running shoes. Even if you didn't get tickets to see the Red Sox (p112), you can have a drink at the Bleacher Bar (p112), which offers a view into Fenway Park. Otherwise, grab drinks at Eastern Standard (p110) before going to hear live music at the House of Blues (p113) or Church (p112).

Top left The magnificent Museum of Fine Arts (p110) **Top right** Trinity Church graces Copley Square (p93)
Bottom The classic redbrick buildings surrounding Harvard Yard exude academia (p116)

FORWARD PLANNING

Three weeks before you go Start walking. Boston is a walking city, so make sure your feet are ready for it. Check the Sox schedule (www.redsox.com) and buy tickets if you can. Log onto Stuff Boston (http://stuffboston.com) to see what's new with food, fashion and culture in the Hub.

One week before you go Buy tickets for the Boston Symphony Orchestra or the theater event of your choice. Check out the WERS concert calendar (http://wers.org) to see what great bands will be playing while you're in town. Make a dinner reservation at L'Espalier (p97) or No 9 Park (p64), and make a booking to see the temporary exhibit at the Museum of Fine Arts (p110).

One day before you go Visit www.boston.com to see the weather forecast. No matter what it says, be sure to pack a sweater.

SNOW DAY

It's bound to happen. We can't deny that it has been known to precipitate in Boston. Fortunately, there is no shortage of fun indoors. Kids can spend all morning frolicking at the Children's Museum (p78), followed by lunch at Flour (p80). If you don't have kids in tow, you'll want to investigate the cutting-edge exhibits at the ICA (p78), with lunch at Sportello (p80). Folks of all ages can wile away the afternoon at the New England Aquarium (p69), since the fish don't seem to be bothered by the weather. Follow up with a film at the Simons IMAX Theatre (p75) and dinner at Bina Osteria (p72).

FOR LOVERS

Every day is Valentine's Day in Boston. If you want to romance your traveling companion, spend the morning at the Isabella Stewart Gardner Museum (p110), a glorious Italian palazzo that is packed with art and perfect for the amorous. Afterwards, you can stroll through the Back Bay Fens (p108) and along the Esplanade (p99), stopping for a picnic lunch along the river. In the afternoon, treat your mate to a ride on the Charles River in an authentic Venetian gondola (p65), complete with a champagne toast. Finish with a sundown drink at Top of the Hub (p92) and a concert by the Boston Symphony Orchestra (p112). Or enjoy a candlelit dinner at a romantic restaurant such as Lala Rokh (p62) or Upstairs on the Square (p119).

FOR STUDENTS

Even the best and brightest are forced to choose: Harvard or MIT. Take a tour of the historic Harvard campus (try the offbeat Unofficial Tour, p167), then visit one of the university's top-notch museums (p116). Alternatively, explore the MIT campus and discover its wealth of public art and innovative architecture (p118), with a visit to the MIT Museum to learn about robots, holograms and other geeky fun. Either way, have lunch at Mr Bartley's Burger Cottage (p119) and spend the afternoon browsing the bookshops and boutiques (p117) in Harvard Sq. When you get hungry, have dinner at Casablanca (p119) or Cambridge, 1 (p119), followed by an edgy performance at the ART (p122).

>NEIGHBORHOODS

The Massachusetts State House (p58)

NEIGHBORHOODS

There was a time when each of Boston's neighborhoods could be described with one adjective: Brahmin Back Bay, Italian North End, Irish South Boston. These days, the neighborhoods are no less distinct, even as they are more diverse.

On the north shore of the Charles River, Charlestown is the site of the original settlement of the Massachusetts Bay Colony; now its streets are lined with redbrick row houses and the historic Navy Yard. The West End is an institutional area dominated by City Hall Plaza and Mass General Hospital, while the narrow streets and Italian accents of the North End still feel like the Old World.

No neighborhood is so quintessential Boston as Beacon Hill, abutted by the Boston Common and topped with the gold-domed Massachusetts State House. On the opposite side of the Common, much of Boston's business and tourist activity takes place Downtown. This is a bustling district crammed with modern skyscrapers and colonial buildings, including the tourist complex at Faneuil Hall and Quincy Market. Across the Fort Point Channel, the Seaport District is a section of South Boston that is fast developing as an attractive waterside destination. The Theater District and Chinatown are overlapping areas, filled with glitzy clubs and theaters and Chinese restaurants for late-night dining.

Back Bay includes the city's most fashionable window-shopping, latte-drinking and people-watching on Newbury St, as well as its most elegant architecture around Copley Sq. Nearby, the Victorian manses in the South End have been claimed by artists and gays, who are creating a vibrant restaurant and gallery scene in the formerly rough-and-tumble neighborhood.

Further west, Kenmore Sq and Fenway attract rowdy club-goers and Red Sox fans, as well as art lovers and culture vultures.

Across the Charles River, Cambridge is a distinct city that boasts two distinguished universities, a host of historic sites and no shortage of artistic, architectural and cultural attractions.

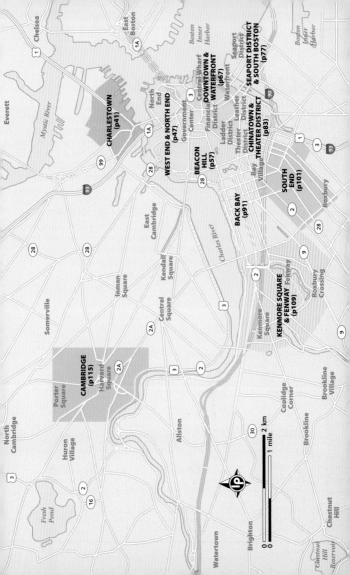

>CHARLESTOWN

Charlestown was settled in the earliest days of the Massachusetts Bay Colony, and some of the revolution's most divisive and bloody fighting took place here. Ultimately, the area was incorporated into Boston in 1873. Despite this common history, Charlestown remains apart. The wide Charles River separates this neighborhood from the rest of the city, preserving its atmosphere as a sort of outlier.

Charlestown has working-class roots. The Charlestown Navy Yard was a thriving ship-building center throughout the 19th and 20th centuries. It closed in 1974, ushering in a new era for the neighborhood. The impressive granite buildings have been transformed into condos and offices, which enjoy a panoramic view of Boston. The narrow streets immediately surrounding Monument Sq are lined with restored 19th-century Federal and Colonial houses, and Main St has a handful of trendy restaurants. Nowadays, it's tourists instead of sailors who come ashore here.

CHARLESTOWN

SEE

◉ BUNKER HILL MONUMENT

☎ 617-242-5641; www.nps.gov/bost;
Monument Sq; admission free; ☼ 9am-
5pm Sep-Jun, to 6pm Jul & Aug;
🚇 Community College

Climb 295 steps to the top of this obelisk to enjoy a panorama of the city and the harbor. The 200ft granite monument tributes the bloody Battle of Bunker Hill, one of the turning points of the revolution. A few relevant exhibits are in the Bunker Hill Museum across the street. This is also the final stop on the Freedom Trail.

◉ GREAT HOUSE SITE

City Sq; ☼ dawn-dusk; 🚇 North Station

A sweet oasis in the midst of Charlestown, City Sq is also an ar-chaeological site. Recent construction unearthed the foundation for a structure called the Great House, widely believed to be John Winthrop's house and the seat of government in 1630.

◉ USS CONSTITUTION

☎ 617-242-2543; www.oldironsides
.com; Charlestown Navy Yard; admission
free; ☼ 10am-6pm Tue-Sun Apr-Oct,
10am-4pm Thu-Sun Nov-Mar; 🚇 North
Station

'Her sides are made of iron!' So cried a crewman as he watched a shot bounce off the thick oak hull of the USS *Constitution* during the War of 1812. This bit of irony earned the legendary ship her nickname. The USS *Constitution* is still the oldest commissioned US Navy ship, dating to 1797.

◉ USS CONSTITUTION MUSEUM

☎ 617-426-1812; www.ussconstitution
museum.org; First Ave, Charlestown
Navy Yard; admission free; ☼ 9am-6pm
Apr-Oct, 10am-5pm Nov-Mar; 🚇 North
Station; ♿

For a play-by-play of the USS *Constitution's* various battles, as well as her current role as the flagship of the US Navy, head indoors to the museum. More interesting is the exhibit on the Barbary War, which explains the birth of the US Navy during this relatively unknown conflict – America's first war at sea.

MISNOMER

Funny thing, the Bunker Hill Monument. It's an odd name for an obelisk that perches atop, um, *Breed's* Hill. In fact, the Battle of Bunker Hill actually took place right here on Breed's Hill too. Apparently Colonel Prescott originally intended to build the rebel fortifications on nearby Bunker Hill, but there was some disagreement and the plans were changed. The name, however, was not. And so it is that one of the crucial battles of the American Revolution was actually a misnomer.

The USS *Constitution* (opposite) is taken out into Boston Harbor once a year, on Independence Day

EAT

FIGS *Pizzeria* $$

☎ 617-242-2229; 67 Main St; ⏲ lunch & dinner; Ⓒ Community College; Ⓥ
This creative pizzeria is the brainchild of celebrity chef Todd English, who tops whisper-thin crusts with interesting, exotic toppings. Case in point: the namesake fig and prosciutto with gorgonzola cheese.

MAX & DYLAN'S
Mediterranean $$

☎ 617-242-7400; www.maxanddylans .com; 1 Chelsea St; ⏲ lunch & dinner; Ⓒ North Station
Classy but casual, this vast space on City Sq is a modern family eatery and trendy bar. The unusual menu has a wide array of sliders (from BBQ pork to Kobe beef), five kinds of mac-n-cheese and an eclectic range of flat-bread sandwiches.

NAVY YARD BISTRO & WINE BAR *French* $$

☎ 617-242-0036; www.navyyardbistro .com; cnr First Ave & Sixth St; ⏲ dinner; Ⓒ North Station
Dark and romantic, this cozy, carved-wood interior is an ideal date destination – perfect for tuna tartare, duck confit or braised shortrib. Pop into the subterranean space behind the Store 24 or take a seat at the pleasant sidewalk seating.

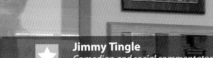

Jimmy Tingle
Comedian and social commentator with a conscience, featured on the Jimmy Tingle for President: The Funniest Campaign in History (2009

What makes Boston so funny? Our streets developed from cow paths, so Bostonians have a twisted, crooked way of looking at things. Plus the constantly changing weather requires a sense of humor. **Best place to see up-and-coming comedic talent** Comedy Studio (p122). **Best place to me funny people** The Burren (p120) or Grendel's Den (p120). **Best example o combining entertainment and social action** The local public radio station WBUR (90.9FM) is committed to this community and caters to an intellectu audience with an excellent lineup of entertainment and political commentary. Other great venues are Club Passim (p122), one of the oldest folk club the country, and the Somerville Theatre (p120), which always features grea bands. **Favorite way to spend a day off** Browsing at the Harvard Booksto (p117), then walking or jogging along the Charles River Esplanade (p99).

¶ TANGIERINO *Moroccan* $$$
☎ 617-242-6009; www.tangierino.com;
83 Main St; ☽ dinner; ⛁ Community
College
This unexpected gem transports
guests from a colonial town
house in historic Charlestown to
a sultan's palace in the Moroccan
desert. Plush pillows and Oriental
carpets on the interior; North African specialties on the menu.

¶ ZUMES COFFEE HOUSE
Café $
☎ 617-242-0038; 223 Main St; ☽ 6am-
6pm Mon-Fri, 7am-6pm Sat & Sun;
⛁ Community College;
Locals love this cozy coffeehouse
for its comfy leather chairs, big
cups of coffee and decadent
doughnuts. Art adorns the walls
and kids keep busy with books
and games.

▼ DRINK

▼ TAVERN ON THE WATER
Historic Pub
☎ 617-242-8040; www.tavernon
thewater.com; 1 Eighth St, Pier 6;
☽ 11:30am-11:30pm, later in summer;
⛁ North Station

Come for the views, the breeze
and the beers (skip the food). Set
at the end of the pier behind the
Navy Yard, this understated tavern
offers one of the finest views of
the Boston harbor and city skyline.

▼ WARREN TAVERN *Pub*
☎ 617-241-8142; www.warrentavern
.com; 2 Pleasant St; ☽ 11:15am-1am;
⛁ Community College
One of the oldest pubs in Boston,
the Warren Tavern has been pour-
ing pints for its customers since
George Washington and Paul
Revere drank here. It is named for
General Joseph Warren, a fallen
hero of the Battle of Bunker Hill
(shortly after which – in 1780 –
this pub was opened).

PLAY

☆ COURAGEOUS SAILING
Outdoor Activities
☎ 617-242-3821; www.courageoussail
ing.org; 1 First Ave; ⛁ North Station
Sailing, take me away on the
Boston Harbor. Small-group lessons are $250 for four three-hour
sessions; also includes one-month
unlimited membership. Private
lessons are $75 per hour.

>WEST END & NORTH END

It was here, at his clapboard house, that Paul Revere commenced that fateful ride 'on the eighteenth of April in Seventy-five.' It was here, high in the Old North Church, that two lanterns were hung to signal to the Minutemen the march of the Redcoats. So it is to here that modern visitors traipse, following the red-brick Freedom Trail past these historic sites.

The neighborhood has changed a lot since the 1700s. In the following centuries, Italian immigrants arrived, turning the North End into Boston's own Lo Stivale (The Boot). Nowadays, the narrow streets are lined with *ristoranti* (restaurants) and *enoteche* (wine bars); it's not unusual to hear old-timers having passionate discussions in the mother tongue.

Nearby, the old West End did not fare so well, nearly eliminated by a devastating case of urban renewal in the 1960s. But the completion of the Big Dig (p156) has prompted a revival of sorts, as both neighborhoods rejoin the rest of Boston.

WEST END & NORTH END

SEE

COPP'S HILL BURYING GROUND

Hull St; 🚇 Haymarket

Dating to 1660, the city's second-oldest cemetery is named for William Copp, who originally owned this land. The oldest graves belong to his children, but this tiny plot of land is also the final resting place for an estimated 10,000 souls, including more than a thousand free blacks who lived in the North End.

MUSEUM OF SCIENCE

☎ 617-723-2500; www.mos.org; Science Park, Charles River Dam; adult/child/senior $19/16/17; 🕙 9am-5pm Sat-Thu Sep-Jun, to 7pm Jul & Aug, to 9pm Fri year-round; 🚇 Science Park; 🅿 🚻 🎒

Let the children frolic freely in this educational playground, filled with hundreds of interactive exhibits. Your kid can make a map of their bedroom in the cartographer's workshop; design a fish to swim in the virtual fish tank; or pet the scaly skin of a snake at a live science demonstration.

OLD NORTH CHURCH

☎ 617-523-6676; www.oldnorth.com; 193 Salem St; donation $1, tours adult/child/senior & student $8/5/6; 🕙 10am-4pm Tue-Sun Jan & Feb, daily 9am-5pm Mar-May, 9am-6pm Jun-Oct, 10am-5pm Nov & Dec; 🚇 Haymarket

Dating to 1723, Boston's oldest church is famous for its revolutionary role. On the night of April 18, 1775, the church sexton hung two lanterns from this steeple, signaling that the British would march on Lexington and Concord via the sea route. Henry Wadsworth Longfellow later memorialized the event in his poem *Paul Revere's Ride*.

PAUL REVERE HOUSE

☎ 617-523-2338; www.paulreverehouse.org; 19 North Sq; adult/child/senior & student $3.50/1/3; 🕙 9:30am-5:15pm mid-Apr–Oct, to 4:15pm Nov–mid-Apr, closed Mon Jan-Mar; 🚇 Haymarket; 🚻 🎒

The oldest house in Boston today – built in 1680 – once belonged to patriot Paul Revere. Take the self-guided tour to get a glimpse of day-to-day life for the silversmith and his 16 children.

SHOP

ART-MOSPHERE GALLERY
Art Gallery

☎ 617-720-4278; www.artmosphereinternational.com; 28½ Prince St; 🚇 Haymarket

Wander away from Hanover St to discover a new perspective on the North End. This gallery specializes in local artists and their depictions of Boston landmarks. Photos, prints and paintings of your favorite

North End eateries make a great souvenir.

☐ CASA DI STILE
Women's Clothing

☎ 857-233-4885; www.casadistile.com; 371 Hanover St; ⏰ 11am-7pm Mon-Sat, noon-6pm Sun; 🚇 Haymarket

This is the new North End, evoking the Italy of high fashion and high heels. If you're in 'relentless pursuit of the favorite top,' then the 'House of Style' is for you, carrying blouses and shirts by dozens of designers.

☐ IN-JEAN-IUS *Jeans*

☎ 617-523-5326; www.injeanius.com; 441 Hanover St; ⏰ 11am-8pm Mon-Fri, 10am-7pm Sat, noon-6pm Sun; 🚇 Haymarket

Shelves are stacked high with loads of designer denims, not to mention snazzy shirts and sweaters to top them off. Maybe those skinny jeans will provide the incentive you need to limit your pasta intake. If you're in the market for evening wear, head around the corner to the sister store, **Twilight** (☎ 617-523-8008; 12 Fleet St).

☐ MODA *Sportswear*

☎ 617-227-6632; 57 Salem St; ⏰ noon-7pm Mon-Fri, 11am-8pm Sat, noon-6pm Sun; 🚇 Haymarket

Boston's most stylish sun salutations occur right here in the North End. Suit up at Moda before head-ing over to the sister studio, North End Yoga (www.northendyoga .com).

☐ NORTH BENNET STREET SCHOOL *Arts & Crafts*

☎ 617-227-1055; www.nbss.org; 39 North Bennet St; ⏰ 10am-2pm Mon-Thu, to 3pm Sat; 🚇 Haymarket

The century-old North Bennet Street School trains its students in traditional crafts such as bookbind-ing, engraving and wood carving. All the jewelry, journals and furni-ture at this gallery are handmade by the artisans in residence.

☐ NORTH END GALLERY
Art Gallery

☎ 617-742-6611; www.northendgallery .com; 354 Hanover St; 🚇 Haymarket

Whether you are in the market for original artwork, limited-edition prints or unique postcards, there is no shortage of cityscapes, street scenes and other artistic render-ings of your favorite New England neighborhoods here.

☐ SHAKE THE TREE
Clothing & Accessories

☎ 617-742-0484; www.shakethetree boston.com; 67 Salem St; ⏰ 11am-7pm; 🚇 Haymarket

You can't know what you will find at this sweet boutique, but it's bound to be good. The little shop carries a wonderful, eclectic assortment of jewelry, stationery, handbags, clothing and house wares.

🛍 VELVET FLY
Secondhand Clothing, Clothing & Accessories

☎ 617-557-4359; www.thevelvetfly.com; 424 Hanover St; ⏰ noon-7pm Mon-Tue, 11am-8pm Wed-Sat, noon-5pm Sun; 🚇 Haymarket

Quaint but cool, trendy but time-less. There are styles both vintage and modern. Most importantly, the unique boutique is fashion-able but still friendly. Superfly owners BethAnn and Lorrinda add a personal touch.

🍴 EAT

🍴 CARMEN *Italian* $$$
☎ 617-742-6421; www.carmenboston .com; 33 North Sq; ⏰ 5:30-10pm Tue-Thu, noon-11pm Fri & Sat, 3-10pm Sun; 🚇 Haymarket

The small space and intimate atmosphere make Carmen one of the city's most romantic restaurants. It's right next door to Paul Revere's House. The modern menu of small plates and seasonal specialties receives rave reviews. Make a reservation or snag a seat at the wine bar and be prepared to wait.

🍴 FLAT IRON
Small Plates & International $$
☎ 617-778-2900; www.flatironboston .com; 119 Merrimac St; ⏰ 5:30-11pm; 🚇 North Station

Named for its triangle-shaped building – also housing the Bulfinch Hotel – this hip eatery adds some international flare to the otherwise bland West End dining scene. It's not exactly tapas, as it claims, but rather an eclectic array of small plates, ranging from seaweed salad to Kobe beef sliders, and an equally interesting cocktail menu.

TUTTO ITALIANO
Foodies flock to the North End specialty shops to stock up on extra virgin olive oil, aged balsamic vinegar, rich roasted coffee beans and other ingredients imported from Italy. Try these local faves:
Polcari's Coffee (☎ 617-227-0786; 105 Salem St; ⏰ 10am-6pm Mon-Sat; 🚇 Haymarket)
Salumeria Italiana (☎ 617-523-8743; www.salumeriaitaliana.com; 151 Richmond Street; 🚇 Haymarket)
Tutto Italiano (☎ 617-557-4002; www.tuttoitalianonorthend.com; 20 Fleet St; ⏰ 10am-7pm Tue-Sat, 9am-3pm Sun; 🚇 Haymarket)

Boston's legendary seafood takes center stage at Giacomo's Ristorante

🍴 GALLERIA UMBERTO

Pizzeria $

☎ 617-227-5709; 289 Hanover St;
🕙 11am-2:30pm Mon-Sat;
🚇 Haymarket

This lunchtime legend closes as soon as the slices of Sicilian are gone, so arrive early to make sure you get yours.

🍴 GIACOMO'S RISTORANTE

Italian $$

☎ 617-523-9026; 355 Hanover St;
🕙 5-10pm; 🚇 Haymarket

Pick a pasta, pick a seafood and pick a sauce. That's the basic concept at Giacomo's, which often has

patrons waiting on the sidewalk for the doors to open. The menu also features delectable fried calamari, a spicy Zuppa di Pesce and an array of excellent specials.

🍴 GREZZO *Raw Food* $$$

☎ 857-362-7288; www.grezzorestaurant
.com; 69 Prince St; 🕙 lunch Tue, lunch &
dinner Wed-Sun; 🚇 Haymarket; Ⓥ

Grezzo is indeed Italian, but don't be confused. In fact, *grezzo* means 'raw,' and this is Boston's first restaurant specializing in vegan raw and living food. The food is creative, surprising and a pleasure to eat. The waitstaff is very knowledgeable, which is crucial, as just about every item on the weekly changing menu requires an explanation.

🍴 NEPTUNE OYSTER
Seafood $$$
☎ 617-742-3474; www.neptuneoyster.com; 63 Salem St; ⏰ 11:30am-11pm Sun-Wed, to midnight Thu-Sat; 🚇 Haymarket

Neptune breaks the North End mold with its retro interior, convivial atmosphere and impressive raw bar. While there are a few Italian entrées, the focus here is seafood, with a small but varied menu featuring pan-seared scallops, grilled fish and lots of lobster.

🍴 NOLLE VOLLE *Sandwiches* $
☎ 617-523-0003; 351 Hanover St; ⏰ 11am-3pm; 🚇 Haymarket

Apparently, *nolle volle* is Latin for 'willy-nilly,' but there is nothing haphazard about this much beloved North End sandwich shop. Black-slate tables and pressed-tin walls adorn the simple, small space. The chalkboard menu features fresh salads, delicious flatbread sandwiches ($8 to $10) and dark, delicious coffee. A perfect lunchtime stop along the Freedom Trail.

🍴 OSTERIA RUSTICO *Italian* $
☎ 617-742-8770; 85 Canal St; ⏰ 9am-3pm Mon-Sat; 🚇 North Station

The West End's best-kept secret. If you're in the neighborhood for breakfast or lunch, you can't do better than little-known Italian eatery Osteria Rustico, which serves super subs and salads, and plentiful pasta dishes.

🍴 PIZZERIA REGINA *Pizzeria* $
☎ 617-227-0765; www.pizzeriaregina.com; 11½ Thacher St; ⏰ 11am-11pm; 🚇 Haymarket

The grandmother of North End pizzerias is famous for brusque but endearing waiters and crispy, thin-crust Neapolitan pizza. Be prepared to wait for a table.

🍴 POMODORO *Italian* $$$
☎ 617-367-4348; 319 Hanover St; ⏰ 5-11pm Tue-Sun; 🚇 Haymarket

After a small-scale renovation, this hole-in-the-wall on Hanover is still one of the North End's most romantic settings. The food is simply but perfectly prepared, while top-notch service guarantees your wine glass is always full. Credit cards are not accepted and there's no restroom, but that's all part of the charm.

🍴 RISTORANTE DAMIANO
Italian & Small Plates $$
☎ 617-742-0020; www.ristorantedamiano.com; 307-309 Hanover St; ⏰ 5-11pm Tue-Fri, noon-midnight Sat, noon-9pm Sun; 🚇 Haymarket

If you can't stomach the thought of a huge plate of pasta and a bottle of wine, head to this contemporary Sicilian café for *piattini* (small plates; $10 to $15) and wine served by the glass. The large windows and an open kitchen make it a cool contrast to the old-fashioned eateries on Hanover St.

TRATTORIA IL PANINO
Italian $$$
☎ 617-720-5720; 11 Parmenter St; 🕑 11am-midnight; 🚇 Haymarket
The portions are healthy, the flavors are delectable and the sweet-talking, Italian-accented waiters are charming indeed. But the most enticing feature of Il Panino is the *giardino,* one of the North End's only options for alfresco dining.

DRINK

ALIBI *Cocktail Lounge*
☎ 617-241-1144; www.alibiboston.com; 215 Charles St, Liberty Hotel; 🕑 5pm-2am; 🚇 Charles/MGH
Set in the former 'drunk tank' of the Charles St jail, Alibi has mug shots hanging on the brick walls and iron bars on the doors and windows. Upstairs and upscale, Clink is set under the soaring ceiling in Liberty Hotel's lobby.

BOSTON BEER WORKS
Microbrewery & Sports Bar
☎ 617-896-2337; 112 Canal St; 🕑 11:30-1am; 🚇 North Station
Boston's own microbrewery is a popular spot for drinking and eating before (or after) a game at the Garden (p55). The addictive french

NEW LIFE FOR LIBERTY
When the Charles St jail first opened in 1851, it was a shining example of the contemporary principles of humanitarian incarceration. All the coolest criminals resided here, including the anarchists Sacco and Vanzetti, black liberationist Malcolm X and Boston's own James Michael Curley.

The good times did not last, however. By the middle of the 20th century, the building was overcrowded, conditions were miserable and there was a constant threat of revolt. On one occasion, two men found bugs in their soup and incited an uprising that would cause $250,000 in damage.

Finally, a group of inmates brought a lawsuit against the county. In 1974 Judge Arthur Garrity actually spent a night in the prison before deciding that the conditions were unacceptable and the prison should be closed immediately.

Twenty years and $16 million later, the former jail is now the luxurious **Liberty Hotel**. These days it houses much more willing residents, no doubt.

fries offer a perfect complement to the revolving menu of seasonal microbrews.

CAFFÉ DELLO SPORT
Italian Café & Sports Bar

☎ 617-523-5063; www.caffedellosport.us; 308 Hanover St; ⏰ 6am-midnight; ⓜ Haymarket

An informal crowd of thick-accented guys from the 'hood sit at glass-topped tables and drink coffee and Campari.

CAFFE VITTORIA *Café*

☎ 617-227-7606; 290-296 Hanover St; ⏰ 7am-midnight Sun-Thu, to 12:30am Fri & Sat; ⓜ Haymarket

Satisfy your sweet tooth with a cappuccino and cannoli or – even better – a well-aged port. Take a seat at a marble-topped table, amidst black-and-white photos and antique furnishings, and sip your prize in Victorian style.

JOHNNIE'S ON THE SIDE
Sports Bar

☎ 617-227-1588; www.johnnieontheside.com; 138 Portland St; ⏰ noon-midnight Mon-Thu, to 2am Fri & Sat, 11am-4pm Sun brunch; ⓜ North Station

Despite the leather furniture and picture windows, this West End newcomer cannot escape the fact that it's a sports bar, with flat-screen TVs and sports paraphernalia adorning the walls. But it's a sports bar for grown-ups, with a good wine list and cocktail selection.

⭐ PLAY

IMPROV ASYLUM *Comedy*

☎ 617-263-6887; www.improvasylum.com; 216 Hanover St; tickets $20; ⓜ Haymarket

No topic is too touchy for this darkly funny improv group. Usu-

---

NORTH END WALKING TOURS

Want a local foodie's opinion about the best place to buy cheese and wine? Want to hear the legends that haunt the North End? Sign up for one of these entertaining walking tours.
Michele Topor's North End Market Tours (☎ 617-523-6032; www.northendmarkettours.com; tours $50; ⏰ 10am & 2pm Wed & Sat, 10am & 3pm Fri) This three-hour tour around the North End includes shopping in a *salumeria* (deli), sampling pastries at the local *pasticceria* (pastry store) and touring an *enoteca* (wine bar).
Secret Tour (☎ 617-720-2283; www.northendsecrettours.com; tours $30; ⏰ 10am, 1pm & 4pm Fri & Sat) This two-hour tour begins at North Sq – opposite Paul Revere's House – and explores the North End's hidden courtyards and passageways, thus uncovering the neighborhood's checkered past.

Dolce, dolce, dolce: Caffe Vittoria (opposite) makes life a little sweeter with cappuccino and cannoli

ally audience members throw out ideas and the cast is off and running – nobody knows where. On Thursday nights at 7pm, a pasta buffet is included in the price of a ticket.

MUGAR OMNI THEATER
Cinema

☎ 617-723-2500; www.mos.org; Science Park, Charles River Dam; adult/child/senior $9/7/8; 🚇 Science Park

For IMAX immersion, check out the space- and natural-science-oriented flicks at the Museum of Science's theater. A sweet sound system will help you believe that you're actually roving around Mars.

TD BANKNORTH GARDEN
Spectator Sports

☎ information 617-624-1900, ☎ tickets 617-931-2000; www.tdbanknorthgarden .com; 150 Causeway St; 🚇 North Station

Watch the **Bruins** (www.bostonbruins .com) play ice hockey or the **Celtics** (www.celtics.com) play basketball when they are performing for the hometown crowd. Boston's largest sports arena is also used for big-name concert events, as well as holding the unspectacular **New England Sports Museum** (☎ 617-624-1234; www.sportsmuseum.org; TD Banknorth Garden; adult/child $6/4; 🕑 11am-2pm game days, to 3pm nongame days).

>BEACON HILL

If you ever wondered why Boston is called 'the Hub,' look no further than Beacon Hill, a Victorian-era neighborhood packed with history, architecture and gobs of charm.

Wandering around Beacon Hill whisks you back about 150 years. The narrow cobblestone streets are still lit with gas lanterns; the distinguished brick town houses are decked with purple windowpanes and blooming flower boxes. Back in the day, Boston's most progressive thinkers held literary salons and abolitionist meetings in these stately mansions. The jewel that crowns the hilltop is the gold-domed State House (p58), the hub of the neighborhood.

Traversing the flat of the hill, Charles St is Boston's most enchanting spot for browsing boutiques and haggling over antiques. A steaming cappuccino is all the more satisfying, a fine dinner all the more romantic, when enjoyed in this delightful setting.

BEACON HILL

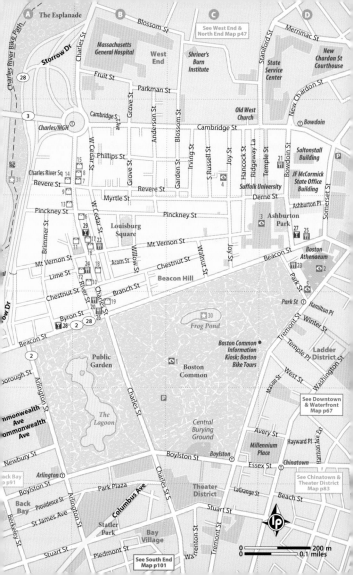

NEIGHBORHOODS

BEACON HILL

SEE

BOSTON COMMON
The 50-acre Boston Common is the country's oldest public park. If you have any doubt, refer to the plaque emblazoned with the words of the treaty between Governor Winthrop and William Blaxton, who sold the land for £30 in 1634. The Common has served many purposes over the years, including as a campground for British troops during the Revolutionary War and providing green grass for cattle grazing until 1830. Although there is still a grazing ordinance on the books, the Common today serves picnickers, sunbathers and people-watchers. In winter, the Frog Pond (p65) attracts ice-skaters, while summer draws theater lovers for Shakespeare on the Common. This is also the starting point for the Freedom Trail.

GRANARY BURYING GROUND
Tremont St; admission free;
⏰ 9am-5pm; 🚇 Park St
Dating to 1660, this atmospheric atoll is crammed with historic headstones, many with creepy carvings. It is the final resting place of all your favorite revolutionary heroes including Paul Revere, Samuel Adams, John Hancock and James Otis.

MASSACHUSETTS STATE HOUSE
☎ 617-727-3676; www.sec.state.ma.us; cnr Beacon & Bowdoin Sts; admission free; ⏰ 9am-5pm, tours 10am-4pm Mon-Fri; 🚇 Park St; ♿ 👶
Charles Bulfinch designed the commanding state capitol, but it was Oliver Wendell Holmes who called it 'the hub of the solar system' (thus earning Boston the nickname 'the Hub'). Here, the

BLACK HERITAGE TRAIL
Learn more about the history of the abolitionist movement and the African American settlement on Beacon Hill by taking a walk along the 1.6-mile Black Heritage Trail. The National Park Service (NPS) conducts guided tours in summer, but maps and descriptions for self-guided tours are available at the **Museum of Afro-American History** (opposite).
> Pay your respects to Robert Gould Shaw, the commander of the 54th Regiment of the Union Army (the nation's first all-black regiment in the Civil War).
> See the houses that provided shelter for runaway slaves.
> Visit Boston's first schools to educate black students.
> See where abolitionists, including William Lloyd Garrison and Frederick Douglass, rallied against racism.

Make a splash in the Boston Common Frog Pond (opposite; p65)

Massachusetts legislators attempt to turn ideas into policy, overseen by a Sacred Cod. Free tours are led by knowledgeable Doric Docents.

MUSEUM OF AFRO-AMERICAN HISTORY
☎ 617-725-0022; www.afroammuseum.org; 46 Joy St; donation $5; ⏱ 10am-4pm Mon-Sat; 🚇 Park St; ♿

Beacon Hill was never the exclusive domain of blue-blood Brahmins. Waves of African Americans, freed from slavery, settled on the back side of the hill, which became a hotbed of abolitionist activity. Occupying the old African Meeting House, this museum remembers the historic events leading up to the Civil War.

PARK STREET CHURCH
☎ 617-523-3383; www.parkstreet.org; 1 Park St; ⏱ 9:30am-3:30pm Tue-Sat mid-Jun–Aug; 🚇 Park St

The 217ft steeple is a Boston landmark, marking the spot of 'Brimstone corner.' It's an apt name for a location that saw William Lloyd Garrison rallying against slavery and Samuel Francis Smith singing 'My Country Tis of Thee.'

Bostonians worship the Park Street Church (p59)

SHOP

BEACON HILL CHOCOLATES
Food & Drink

☎ 617-725-1900; www.beaconhill chocolates.com; 92 Pinckney St; 🚇 Charles/MGH

Using decoupage to afix old post-cards, photos and illustrations, these gift boxes are works of art even before they are filled with truffles. Pick out an image of historic Boston as a souvenir for the sweet tooth in your life.

BOSTON RUNNING CO
Sportswear

☎ 617-723-2786; www.bostonrunning company.com; 121 Charles St; 🕙 11am-7pm Mon & Wed-Fri, to 2:30pm Tue, to 5pm Sat & Sun; 🚇 Charles/MGH

Marathon record-holder and former Olympic athlete Mike Roche brings his expertise to average-joe-runner, with 'video gait analysis'. All footwear and apparel meet his rigorous requirements.

CIBELINE
Women's Clothing & Accessories

☎ 617-742-0244; www.cibelinesariano .com; 120 Charles St; 🕙 11am-7pm Tue & Wed, 11:30am-7:30pm Thu & Fri, 10am-6pm Sat, noon-5pm Sun; 🚇 Charles/MGH

Local designer Cibeline Sariano's Hepburn-inspired styles include gorgeous gowns, classic jackets, and fun, fresh skirts and slacks.

CORE DE VIE *Sportswear*

☎ 617-720 0411; www.coredevie.com; 40 Charles St; 🚇 Charles/MGH

The main reason to come to Core de Vie is its excellent, ever-renewing selection of lululemon active wear, but you'll also find versatile, comfortable clothing that you can wear in your everyday life.

CRUSH BOUTIQUE
Women's Clothing

☎ 617-720 0010; www.shopcrush boutique.com; 131 Charles St;

⏱ 10am-7pm Mon-Sat, noon-6pm Sun; Ⓣ Charles/MGH

Fashion mavens rave about this cute, cozy, basement boutique on Charles St, which is packed with dresses, tops, pants and jewelry – mostly by NY and LA designers that are not often seen on the streets of Boston.

FRENCH DRESSING
Lingerie

☎ 617-723-4968; www.frenchdressing lingerie.com; 49 River St; ⏱ 11am-7pm Tue-Fri, to 6pm Sat, noon-5pm Sun; Ⓣ Charles/MGH

Putting the French accent in 'lingerie,' this sweet spot, decorated with crystal chandeliers and paisley prints, sells light and lacy underthings, as well as luxurious loungewear. Ooh la la.

HELEN'S LEATHER
Shoes & Accessories

☎ 617-742-2077; www.helensleather .com; 110 Charles St; ⏱ 10am-6pm Mon-Wed, Fri & Sat, to 8pm Thu, noon-6pm Sun; Ⓣ Charles/MGH

These boots are made for walking. Dressy boots, work boots and yes, even cowboy boots. Helen's has an incredible selection for every occasion, not to mention sandals, jackets, handbags and other soft, supple leather accessories.

PIXIE STIX
Children's Clothing

☎ 617-523-3211; www.pixiestixboston .com; 131 Charles St; ⏱ 10am-6pm Mon, Tue & Sat, to 7pm Wed-Fri, noon-6pm Sun; Ⓣ Charles/MGH

This sweet boutique caters to 'tweens' – that awkward age

ANTIQUE ROAD

There was a time when Beacon Hill was populated with antique shops and nothing else: some historians claim that the country's antique trade began right here. There is still enough old stuff to thrill the *Antiques Roadshow* lover in you, with dozens of antique shops lining Charles St and nearby River St. Here are a few of our favorites.

Boston Antique Company (☎ 617-227-9810; 119 Charles St; ⏱ 10am-6pm Mon-Sat, noon-6pm Sun; Ⓣ Charles/MGH) Filled to the brim with furniture, porcelain, jewelry, textiles and paintings, much of it from area estates.

Eugene Galleries (☎ 617-227-3062; 76 Charles St; Ⓣ Charles/MGH) Specializing in antique maps and prints.

Marika's Antique Shop (☎ 617-523-4520; 130 Charles St; Ⓣ Charles/MGH) For 50 years and counting, Marika's has carried an excellent selection of jewelry, beads and pocket watches.

Twentieth Century Ltd (☎ 617-742-1031; www.boston-vintagejewelry.com; 73 Charles St; Ⓣ Charles St/MGH) This place sells the stuff that we wish we would inherit from our grandmothers, including costume jewelry made by the great designers of yesteryear.

between kid and teenager – and does so with cuteness *and* coolness, if that's possible. The fun fashions at Pixie Stix will appeal to mother and daughter with bright colors, bold patterns and preppy styles.

RED WAGON
Children's Clothing

☎ 617-523-9402; www.theredwagon .com; 69 Charles St; ⏰ 10am-6pm Mon, Tue & Sat, to 7pm Wed-Fri, noon-6pm Sun; 🚇 Charles/MGH

The Red Wagon carries equally adorable outfits for smaller tykes, not to mention books, toys and many gift options for newborns.

☐ WISH *Women's Clothing*

☎ 617-227-4441; www.wishboston .com; 49 Charles St; ⏰ 10am-6pm Mon, Tue & Sat, to 7pm Wed-Fri, noon-6pm Sun; 🚇 Charles/MGH

Come here to splurge on a special-occasion gown. Or stroll down the street to **Wish Splash** (☎ 617-228-0225; 15 Charles St) to splurge on a special-occasion swimsuit.

🍴 EAT

🍴 BIN 26 ENOTECA
Italian & Wine Bar　　　　　$$$

☎ 617-723-5939; www.bin26.com; 26 Charles St; ⏰ lunch Mon-Sat, dinner daily; 🚇 Charles/MGH

The Bin is all about the *vin,* as you'll see from the wine-bottle-

themed décor. The extensive wine list includes some fancy bottles that are likely out of your price range, as well as a moderately priced house wine that is bottled in Italy just for the restaurant. Reservations recommended.

🍴 GROTTO
Italian　　　　　　　　　　$$

☎ 617-227-3434; www.grottorestaurant .com; 37 Bowdoin St; ⏰ lunch Mon-Fri, dinner daily; 🚇 Bowdoin

This cozy basement-level place is tucked into the back side of Beacon Hill. The menu often changes but the tried-and-true spaghetti and meatballs is hard to resist, thanks to 'insanely fabulous tomato sauce.' Reservations are recommended.

🍴 LALA ROKH
Persian　　　　　　　　　$$$

☎ 617-720-5511; www.lalarokh.com; 97 Mt Vernon St; ⏰ lunch Mon-Fri, dinner daily; 🚇 Charles/MGH

Named for a beautiful, fantastical Persian princess, Lala Rokh has a romantic, exotic interpretation of Middle Eastern cuisine. While the ingredients will be familiar to fans of this cuisine, the subtle innovations – an aromatic spice here or savory herb there – set this cooking apart. Reservations recommended.

Barbara Lynch
Celebrity chef, owner of fabulous food venues including No 9 Park, B&G Oysters, Sportello and Drink, Southie native

How has Boston dining changed in recent years? More fine dining, more bistro food, vast improvements in wine, service and hospitality. **Favorite holdovers from yesteryear?** Snap dogs from Sully's at Castle Island (p78), fried clams from clam shacks in Ipswich. **What is unique about Boston cuisine?** Seafood! **Where to sample it?** B&G Oysters (p103), Jasper White's Summer Shack (p97). **New trends in Boston dining** Bakeries such as Nolle Volle (p52). Also, the revival of the art of the cocktail, like we are doing at Drink (p81). **Best places for foodies to shop** South End Formaggio (p105), Butcher Shop (p105), Salumeria Italiana (p50) and Cheng Kwong Market (p84). Louis Boston (p95) is good for gifts and kitchenware. **Best time of year to eat in Boston** Summertime is best for fresh produce, rooftop barbecues and picnics on the Esplanade (p99).

⅋ NO 9 PARK *European* $$$
☎ 617-742-9991; www.no9park.com;
9 Park St; ☯ lunch & dinner Mon-Fri,
dinner Sat; 🚇 Park St; Ⓟ
Chef-owner Barbara Lynch has
been lauded by food and wine
magazines for her delectable
French and Italian culinary masterpieces and her first-rate wine list.
Now she has cast her celebrity-
chef spell all around town, but this
is the place that made her famous.
Reservations required; parking
costs $16.

⅋ PARAMOUNT
Cafeteria & American $
☎ 617-720-1152; www.paramount
boston.com; 44 Charles St; ☯ breakfast,
lunch & dinner; 🚇 Charles/MGH
Since 1937, hungry Bostonians
have been hunkering down at the
Paramount. By day, it's an old-
fashioned cafeteria serving breakfast fare, burgers and big salads.
For dinner, the place goes upscale
with table service and candlelight.

⅋ SCOLLAY SQUARE
American $$
☎ 617-742-4900; www.scollaysquare
.com; 21 Beacon St; ☯ lunch & dinner
Mon-Fri, dinner Sat, brunch & dinner Sun;
🚇 Park St
This retro restaurant hearkens
back to the glory days of Scollay
Sq, which used to sit up the road.
Old photos and memorabilia

adorn the walls, including a series
of burlesque beauties peering out
from behind the bar.

⅋ UPPER CRUST *Pizzeria* $
☎ 617-723-9600; 20 Charles St;
☯ lunch & dinner; 🚇 Charles/MGH; Ⓥ
This hole-in-the-wall pizza joint
is the original outlet of this local
chain, which is now sprouting up
all around Boston. It's a simple
concept: Neapolitan-style pizza
with a crispy thin crust and fresh,
straightforward toppings.

⅋ ZEN *Japanese, Sushi* $$
☎ 617-371-1230; www.zensushibar.com;
21A Beacon St; ☯ lunch & dinner Mon-
Sat, 2:30-10pm Sun; 🚇 Park St
The minimalist décor and extensive
menu are typical sushi-bar stuff,
but the menu also features mains
such as rack of lamb and soft-shell
crab, as well as items cooked on
the authentic Japanese stone grill.

🍸 DRINK

🍸 21ST AMENDMENT *Pub*
☎ 617-227-7100; www.21stboston.com;
150 Bowdoin St; 🚇 Park St
Named for one of the most
important amendments to the
US Constitution, this tavern has
been an ever-popular haunt for
overeducated and underpaid
statehouse workers to bitch about
the wheels of government.

🍸 CHEERS *Historic Pub*

☎ 617-227-9605; www.cheersboston
.com; 84 Beacon St; 🚇 Arlington

We understand that this is a mandatory pilgrimage place for fans of the TV show. Formerly the Bull & Finch pub, it looks like the TV set from the sidewalk but not on the inside. Unfortunately, nobody knows your name.

🍸 SEVENS ALE HOUSE *Pub*

☎ 617-523-9074; www.sevensalehouse
.com; 77 Charles St; ⏲ noon-1am;
🚇 Charles/MGH

This is old-school Boston, with glasses suspended over a wooden bar and a Flutie jersey hanging on the wall. It's a quintessential neighborhood place where folks come to play chess and shoot the breeze.

★ PLAY

★ BOSTON COMMON FROG POND *Outdoor Activities*

☎ 617-635-2120; www.bostoncommon
frogpond.org; Boston Common; adult/child $4/free; ⏲ 10am-5pm Mon, to 10pm Fri & Sat mid-Nov–mid-Mar, 11am-6pm Jul & Aug; 🚇 Park St; 👶

Splash around in summer, skate around in winter. Skate rentals (adults/children $8/5), lockers and restrooms are available. Weekends are often crowded, as are weekdays around noon, as local skate fiends spend their lunch break on the ice.

★ COMMUNITY BOATING *Outdoor Activities*

☎ 617-523-1038; www.community
-boating.org; Charles River Esplanade; kayaks per day $35, sailboats $75;
⏲ 1pm-dusk Mon-Fri, 9am-dusk Sat & Sun Apr-Oct; 🚇 Charles/MGH; 👶

As long as you can demonstrate your ability, you can borrow the kayaks and sailboats and cruise around the Charles River.

★ GONDOLA DI VENEZIA *Outdoor Activities*

☎ 617-876-2800; www.bostongondolas
.com; Community Boating, Charles River Esplanade; tours per couple $99-229;
🚇 Charles/MGH

Make no mistake about it – the Charles River is not the Grand Canal. However, the gondolier's technique and the craftsmanship of the boat make these private gondola rides a romantic treat.

>DOWNTOWN & WATERFRONT

This is where it all started. Today, it is Boston's hustling, bustling retail and financial center. But 400 years ago, this was the Shawmut Peninsula, where the Puritans built their 'shining city on a hill.'

Formed by the comings and goings of the cows, the well-trodden 17th-century paths gave rise to today's maze of streets. Remnants of Colonial-era architecture – such as the Old State House and Faneuil Hall – are now dwarfed by surrounding skyscrapers. The wharves that once sheltered mercantile ships laden with coffee, tea and spices are now the docking places for harbor cruises and passenger ferries.

This vital, vibrant neighborhood is an incredible example of the marriage between history and progress that so defines Boston. Centuries-old architecture has been reconverted into functional buildings; the Central Artery has been removed, reconnecting the city to its working waterfront; and the neighborhood continues to live and work and thrive.

DOWNTOWN & WATERFRONT

◉ SEE
Boston Massacre Site ...(see 5)
Faneuil Hall **1** D1
King's Chapel &
   Burying Ground **2** C2
National Park Service
   Visitor Center ....(see 5)
New England Aquarium **3** E2
Old South
   Meeting House **4** C2
Old State House **5** C2

☐ SHOP
Bostonian Society
   Museum Shop ......(see 10)
Brattle Book Shop **6** B3
City Sports **7** C3

Filene's Basement **8** C3
Jewelers Exchange
   Building **9** C2
Local Charm **10** D2
London Harness
   Company **11** C3

⑪ EAT
Bertucci's **12** D2
Bina Osteria **13** B4
Chacarero **14** C2
Durgin Park **15** D1
Falafel King ....(see 30)
Haymarket **16** C1
KO Prime **17** B2
Legal Sea Foods **18** E2
Marliave **19** C2
Pressed **20** D2

Quincy Market **21** D1
Sam LaGrassa's **22** C2
Union Oyster House **23** C1

☐ DRINK
JJ Foley's **24** C4
Last Hurrah **25** B2
Silvertone **26** B3
Vault **27** D2

★ PLAY
Codzilla **28** E1
Felt **29** B3
Mojitos **30** B3
Opera House **31** B3
Simons IMAX
   Theatre **32** E2

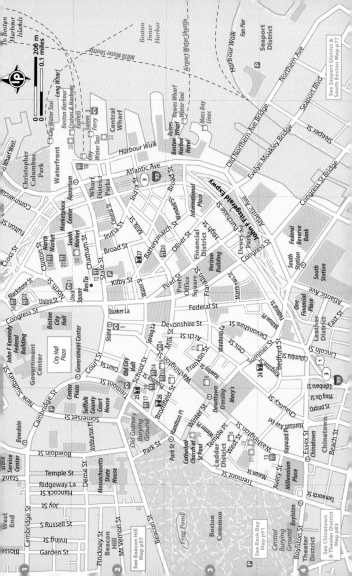

NEIGHBORHOODS

DOWNTOWN & WATERFRONT

SEE

BOSTON HARBOR ISLANDS

☎ 617-223-8666; www.bostonislands
.org; admission free; 🚇 Aquarium; ♿ ♨
Boston Harbor is sprinkled with
34 islands, many of which are
open for trail walking, bird-
watching, fishing and swimming. The islands offer a range
of ecosystems – sandy beaches,
rocky cliffs, fresh and saltwater
marshes and forested trails. **Harbor
Express** (☎ 617-222-6999; 1 Long Wharf,
off Atlantic Ave; round-trip adult/child/senior
$14/8/10; 🕙 9am-5pm mid-Apr–mid-Oct)
offers a seasonal ferry service
from Long Wharf. Purchase a
round-trip ticket to Georges
Island or Spectacle Island, from
where you can catch the interisland water shuttle ($3) to the
smaller islands.

FANEUIL HALL

☎ 617-242-5642; Congress St; admission
free; 🕙 9am-5pm; 🚇 Haymarket or
State; ♿ ♨
Market place and public meeting
space, Faneuil Hall is beloved
for its grasshopper weather
vane. During the revolutionary
period, it was the site of so much
rabblerousing that it earned the
nickname the 'Cradle of Liberty.'
Hear about the building's history
from National Park Service (NPS)
rangers on the 2nd floor.

KING'S CHAPEL & BURYING GROUND

☎ 617-227-2155; www.kings-chapel.org;
58 Tremont St; donation $2; 🕙 10am-
4pm Mon-Sat, 1:30-4pm Sun Jun-Aug,
10am-4pm Sat, 1:30-4pm Sun Sep-May,
services 12:15pm Wed & 11am Sun year-
round; 🚇 Park St or State

ISLAND-HOPPING

Want to spend a day exploring the Harbor Islands? Hop on the first ferry at 9am to Georges
Island, where you can spend about two hours exploring Fort Warren. After lunch, take the
shuttle to Lovells Island to catch some rays on the otherwise empty beach and cool off in the
refreshing Atlantic waters. Spend a few hours on Lovells' rocky shores, but don't miss the after
noon shuttle to Grape Island. Here, you can tag along on the ranger-led 'wild edibles' tour,
or find your own stash of wild berries (but check they are safe to eat). Take the last shuttle
(around 4:30pm) back to Georges Island to catch the ferry to the mainland. A few tips:
> Only Georges and Spectacle Islands have food and water, so you may want to pack a picnic.
> The interisland shuttle runs several times a day, but not every hour. Make sure you
  check the schedule in advance and plan your day accordingly.
> Don't try to visit more than two or three islands in one day: you'll end up spending all
  your time riding or waiting for boats.

Get your hands wet in the New England Aquarium's Edge of the Sea touch tank

The original Anglican church was built on this site in 1688, much to the chagrin of the Puritans. Today, the granite chapel is a lovely place to hear recitals (Tuesday at 12:15pm, $3). The adjacent burying ground is the oldest in the city, with headstones dating to 1623. Among other notables buried here is John Winthrop, the first governor of the fledgling Massachusetts Bay Colony.

NEW ENGLAND AQUARIUM

☎ 617-973-5200; www.neaq.org; Central Wharf; adult/child/senior $20/12/18; 9am-5pm Mon-Thu, to 6pm Fri-Sun, open 1hr later Jul & Aug; Aquarium; P ⑤ ♿

Teeming with sea creatures of all sizes, shapes and colors, this giant fishbowl is an amazing up-close introduction to the sea. Countless exhibits explore the lives and habitats of underwater oddities, including penguins, sharks, jellyfish, turtles and more. Coming soon: a new exhibit featuring sea mammals.

OLD SOUTH MEETING HOUSE

☎ 617-482-6439; www.oldsouth meetinghouse.org; 310 Washington St; adult/child/senior & student $5/1/4; 9:30am-5pm Apr-Oct, 10am-4pm Nov-Mar; Downtown Crossing; ⑤ ♿

Thousands of angry colonists gathered in this brick meeting house to protest the tax the British imposed on tea in 1773. The resulting act – the Boston Tea

Party – led to the city's occupation by British soldiers, and before anyone knew what hit them, the colonists were fighting for independence.

OLD STATE HOUSE & BOSTON MASSACRE SITE

☎ 617-720-3290; www.bostonhistory.org; 206 Washington St; adult/child/senior & student $5/1/4; 🕑 9am-4pm Jan, to 5pm Feb-Jun, to 6pm Jul & Aug; 🚇 State

Boston's oldest public building is tucked in between the busy streets. From this balcony, flanked by lions and unicorns, the Declaration of Independence was first read to Bostonians in 1776. Most dramatically, the seal in front (in the middle of the traffic circle) marks the spot of the Boston Massacre – the revolution's earliest act of violence and first loss of life.

🛍 SHOP

🏬 BOSTONIAN SOCIETY MUSEUM SHOP *Souvenirs*

☎ 617-720-3284; South Market; 🕑 10am-9pm Mon-Sat, noon-6pm Sun; 🚇 State

Americana mania! Look for woven throws featuring flags and eagles, presidential prints and reproductions of Paul Revere's depiction of the Boston Massacre. Not to mention Boston Harbor tea, stars-and-stripes pasta and other treats to enliven your next 4th-of-July cook out.

📖 BRATTLE BOOK SHOP *Bookstore*

☎ 617-542-0210; www.brattlebookshop.com; 9 West St; 🕑 9am-5:30pm Mon-Sat; 🚇 Park St

The Brattle Book Shop has been catering to Boston's literati since 1825. It is a treasure trove

BARGAIN BASEMENT

The granddaddy of bargain stores is **Filene's Basement** (☎ 617-542-2011; www.filenesbasement.com; 426 Washington St). Originally, Filene's sold its overstocked and irregular items in the basement of the flagship store. Shoppers would flock from miles around to browse the heavily discounted merchandise. The store became so popular that Filene's Basement started opening outlets in malls up and down the East Coast. But this is the original, right here on Washington St, in the basement of the original Filene's building (even if Filene's is no longer here). Boston loves Filene's Basement so much that the building is being demolished, rebuilt and converted into condos and hotel space – and Filene's was scheduled to move back into its original space in the basement (plus a few floors above ground, too). Now that's a city that hangs on to its history.

crammed with out-of-print, rare and first-edition books.

CITY SPORTS *Sportswear*
☎ 617-423-2015; www.citysports.com; 11 Bromfield St; 9am-8pm Mon-Fri, 10am-8pm Sat, 11am-7pm Sun; Downtown Crossing

This local chain was founded in 1983 by 'a couple of local joes' who didn't have anywhere to buy sporting goods. Now City Sports sells sports apparel up and down the East Coast. And with that ubiquitous City Sports T-shirt, they don't even need to advertise.

JEWELERS EXCHANGE BUILDING *Jewelry*
333 Washington St; Downtown Crossing

With over 100 jewelers under one roof, this historic building is the first stop for many would-be grooms. There are some jewelers with retail space on the 1st floor, while other less conspicuous artisans work upstairs.

LOCAL CHARM *Jewelry*
☎ 617-723-9796; 2 South Market; State

These days, Quincy Market (p73) is packed with chain stores that you can find anywhere in America. Wouldn't it be nice to experience a little local charm? This tiny jewelry boutique delivers just that. Doing exquisite things with sterling silver and gemstones, the jewelry is tasteful yet artful, interesting and unique. Best of all, it's handmade by local artisans.

LONDON HARNESS COMPANY *Leather Goods*
☎ 617-542-9234; www.londonharness .com; 60 Franklin St; 9:30am-6pm Mon-Fri; Downtown Crossing

Back in 1776, a local saddlemaker joined forces with a well-established trunkmaker, forming a partnership that would claim Ben Franklin as a customer. Although you can't buy saddles here anymore, you can still get high-quality leather and classic styles in handbags, briefcases and suitcases.

EAT

BERTUCCI'S *Pizzeria* $$
☎ 617-227-7889; www.bertuccis.com; 22 Merchants Row; lunch & dinner; Aquarium or State; **V**

Despite its nationwide expansion, Bertucci's remains a Boston favorite for brick-oven pizza. Lunch is a real bargain: all mains come with unlimited salad and fresh, hot rolls.

NEIGHBORHOODS

DOWNTOWN & WATERFRONT

Ever-popular Legal Sea Foods (opposite)

🍴 BINA OSTERIA
Italian & Wine Bar $$$
☎ 617-956-0888; www.binaboston; 581 Washington St; ⏲ 10am-2:30pm & 5pm-midnight Mon-Fri, 5pm-midnight Sat & Sun; 🚇 Downtown Crossing

Normally 'Italian' and 'experimental' don't go together, but here you have the old familiar flavors in unexpected combinations, sometimes topped with unrecognizable foams and gels.

🍴 DURGIN PARK *American* $$
☎ 617-227-2038; www.durgin-park.com; North Market, Faneuil Hall; ⏲ lunch & dinner; 🚇 Haymarket

Durgin Park hasn't changed much since the restaurant opened in 1827. Nor has the menu, which features New England standards such as fish chowder, chicken pot pie and Boston baked beans. Save room for Indian pudding for dessert.

🍴 HAYMARKET
Farmers Market $
Blackstone St; ⏲ 8am-5pm Fri & Sat; 🚇 Haymarket

Touch the produce here and you risk the wrath of the vendors ('They're a friggin' dollar – quit looking at the strawberries and just buy 'em!'). But no one else in the city matches these prices on ripe-and-ready fruits and vegetables.

KO PRIME *Steak* $$$

☎ 617-772-5821; www.koprimeboston
.com; 90 Tremont St; ☼ lunch Mon-Fri,
dinner daily; 🚇 Park St

A sophisticated and stylish steak
house, complete with Holstein-
print furniture and many meaty
delights. The menu features 10
different kinds of steaks, plus bone
marrow, seared foie gras and Kobe
beef tartare.

LEGAL SEA FOODS
Seafood $$

☎ 617-227-3115; www.legalseafoods
.com; 255 State St; ☼ lunch & dinner;
🚇 Aquarium; ♿

You've seen the fresh fish making
wisecracks on the sides of Boston
buses ('Kiss my bass'); now taste
the goods. There are many outlets
around town, but none is more
appropriate than this one on the
waterfront.

MARLIAVE
French & American $$

☎ 617-422-0004; www.marliave.com;
10 Bosworth St; ☼ lunch & dinner;
🚇 Park St; Ⓥ

For a taste of old Boston, head to
this vintage restaurant, replete
with mosaic floors, tin ceilings and
black-and-white photos. PS To get
here, you'll have to climb the Province House steps, the stairway that
once led to the colonial governor's
mansion.

QUINCY MARKET
Food Court $

☎ 617-338-2323; ☼ 10am-9pm
Mon-Sat, noon-6pm Sun; 🚇 Haymarket

Decision-making can be a challenge here – there are about 20
restaurants and 40 food stalls to
choose from. Seating under the
central rotunda.

UNION OYSTER HOUSE
Seafood $$

☎ 617-227-2750; www.unionoyster
house.com; 41 Union St; ☼ lunch &
dinner; 🚇 Haymarket

Daniel Webster ate here. So did
John F Kennedy. The oldest restau-
rant in Boston, ye olde Union
Oyster House has been serving up
seafood in this historic redbrick
building since 1826. Order a dozen
oysters on the half-shell and watch
the shuckers work their age-old
magic.

DRINK

Y JJ FOLEY'S *Irish Pub*

☎ 617-695-2529; 21 Kingston St;
🚇 Downtown Crossing

This delightful dive has been get-
ting the locals liquored up since
1909. Two-dollar beers ensure a
steady stream of regulars, as do
the affable Irish boys behind the
bar. We dare you to ask one of
them to 'PBR me ASAP!'

NEIGHBORHOODS

DOWNTOWN & WATERFRONT

A SANDWICH IS A SANDWICH IS A SANDWICH

For a quick, cheap and delicious lunch, stop by one of these Downtown favorites for a sandwich of sorts:

Chacarero (☎ 617-367-1267; www.chacarero.com; 26 Province St; 🕑 8am-6pm Mon-Fri; 🚇 Downtown Crossing) This traditional Chilean sandwich is made with grilled chicken or beef, Muenster cheese, fresh tomatoes, guacamole and the surprise ingredient – steamed green beans.

Falafel King (☎ 617-338-8355; http://falafelkingboston.com; 48 Winter St; 🕑 11am-8pm Mon-Fri, to 4pm Sat; 🚇 Downtown Crossing; Ⓥ) Two words: free falafels. That's right, everyone gets a little free sample before even ordering.

Pressed (☎ 617-482-9700; www.pressedsandwiches.com; 2 Oliver St; 🕑 breakfast & lunch Mon-Fri; 🚇 Downtown Crossing; Ⓥ) The simple, straightforward menu features almost 20 different sandwiches, all made on fresh bread and pressed in a heated grill.

Sam LaGrassa's (☎ 617-357-6861; www.samlagrassas.com; 44 Province St; 🕑 lunch Mon-Fri; 🚇 Downtown Crossing) In a word, gigantic. You won't be disappointed by the famous Romanian pastrami or the 'fresh from the pot' corned beef.

🍸 LAST HURRAH
Hotel Bar & Lounge
☎ 617-227-8600; www.omnihotels
.com; 60 School St; 🕑 11:30am-12:30am
Mon-Fri, 4:30-11:30pm Sat; 🚇 Park St
The likes of Henry Wadsworth
Longfellow and Ralph Waldo Emerson used to spend their Saturdays
in the lobby bar of the Omni Parker
House. Enjoy a dish of hot nuts
and drink a bourbon, just like they
probably did.

🍸 SILVERTONE *Retro Pub*
☎ 617-338-7887; www.silvertonedown
town.com; 69 Bromfield St; 🕑 11:30am-
2am Mon-Fri, 6pm-2am Sat; 🚇 Park St
Comfort food complements the
old-fashioned diner atmosphere
at this ever-popular basement bar.

It's casual, it's convivial and it's
usually crowded.

🍸 VAULT *Cocktail Lounge*
☎ 617-292-3355; www.thevaultboston
.com; 105 Water St; 🚇 State
In the heart of the Financial District,
the Vault attracts a lively after-work
crowd around 6pm on Wednesday.
Loosen your tie and sip a creative
cocktail. Who can resist Mr Happy?

PLAY

Long Wharf and Central Wharf
are the starting points for
whale-watching cruises to the
Stellwagen Bank National Marine
Sanctuary and sight-seeing cruises
around the Boston Harbor.

⭐ CODZILLA *Outdoor Activities*
☎ 617-227-4320; www.bostonharbor
cruises.com; 1 Long Wharf; adult/
child/senior $25/21/23; ☷ May-Sep;
🚇 Aquarium; ♿

Less of a boat ride and more
of a roller coaster in the waves.
This 2800HP speedboat cruises
through the waves at speeds up to
40mph. Painted like a multicolored
shark with a big toothy grin, the
boat has a unique hull design that
enables it to do the ocean version
of doughnuts.

⭐ FELT *Nightlife*
☎ 617-350-5555; http://feltclubboston
.com; 533 Washington St; ☷ 5pm-2am
Tue-Sat; 🚇 Boylston; 🅿

Nightclub, lounge and billiards
club all in one. There are only
14 pool tables, so there's usually a wait, but there is plenty of
people-watching to do in the
meantime.

⭐ MOJITOS *Nightlife*
☎ 617-988-8123; www.mojitoslounge
.com; 48 Winter St; ☷ 9pm-2am Thu-
Sun; 🚇 Downtown Crossing

Feeling hot, hot, hot? At Mojito's,
you'll find a lounge where house

bands play salsa and timba tunes
(free salsa lessons at 9:15pm most
nights). Downstairs, the dance
club caters to the scantily clad
with hip-hop, Brazilian, reggaeton
and sounds related to the Tropic
of Capricorn.

⭐ OPERA HOUSE *The Arts*
☎ 617-880-2442; 539 Washington St;
🚇 Downtown Crossing

This lavish theater has been restored to its 1928 glory, complete
with a mural-painted ceiling, gold-
gilded molding and plush velvet
curtains. The venue regularly hosts
productions from the Broadway
Across America series, as well as
performances by the **Boston Ballet**
(www.bostonballet.org).

⭐ SIMONS IMAX THEATRE
Cinema
☎ 617-973-5200; www.neaq.org;
Central Wharf; adult/senior & child $9/8;
🚇 Aquarium

At the New England Aquarium,
this IMAX bad boy plays nature
films on a six-story screen, in 3D.
That way when you have a gander
at *Sharks*, you'll actually feel like
you're about to be eaten.

>SEAPORT DISTRICT & SOUTH BOSTON

South Boston has gotten a bad rap over the years, suffering from a history of xenophobia and a legacy of the Boston mob. But the old Irish neighborhood is emerging from under its shroud, as Southie becomes more diverse and more dynamic. Frankly, it's hard to resist the city's best beaches and glorious harbor views, not to mention the unbeatable lineup of Irish pubs.

Nowhere in Boston has seen more change than the Seaport District, the oddly shaped harbor-side neighborhood that is wedged in between South Boston and the Fort Point Channel. Once abandoned to artists and fisherfolk, the Seaport District is now the target of an ambitious development project, as evidenced by the huge convention center, several luxury hotels and – the centerpiece – the new Institute of Contemporary Art (ICA) on the water's edge. Now, even Mayor Menino wants to move his office here.

SEAPORT DISTRICT & SOUTH BOSTON

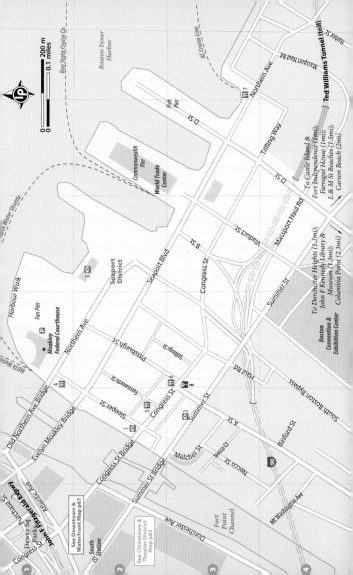

Bay State Cruise Co

Boston Inner
Harbour

AC Cruise Line

200 m
0.1 miles

Fish
Pier

Commonwealth
Pier

World Trade
Center

Northern Ave

Ted Williams Tunnel (toll)

Massport Haul Rd

Harbor St

To Castle Island &
Fort Independence (1mi);
Farragut House (1mi);
L & M St Beaches (1.5mi);
Carson Beach (2mi)

Trilling Way

D St

D St

Massport Haul Rd

Viaduct St

B St

Seaport Blvd

Seaport
District

Congress St

Summer St

To Dorchester Hghts (1.3mi);
John F Kenndy Library &
Museum (1.3mi);
Columbia Point (2.3mi)

Boston
Convention &
Exhibition Center

South Boston Bypass

Haul Rd

MBTA Water Shuttle

Harbour Walk

Moakley
Federal Courthouse

Fan Pier

P

Northern Ave

Pittsburgh St

Stillings St

Farnsworth St

Congress St

Summer St

A St

Binford St

Old Northern Ave Bridge

Evelyn Moakley Bridge

Sleeper St

Congress St Bridge

Summer St Bridge

Melcher St

Necco Ct

Necco St

Mt Washington Ave

John Fitzgerald Expwy

Dewey Sq

Purchase St

Congress St

Atlantic Ave

South
Station

See Downtown &
Waterfront Map p67

See Chinatown &
Theater District
Map p83

Dorchester Ave

Fort Point
Channel

SEE

CASTLE ISLAND & FORT INDEPENDENCE

☎ 617-727-5290; Marine Park;
🕐 dawn-dusk May-Sep; 🚇 Broadway;
🅿 ♿

Since 1634, eight different fortresses have occupied this strategic spot at the entrance to the Inner Harbor. Today, Fort Independence sits on 22 acres of parkland, with a paved pathway following the perimeter of the peninsula. Great for picnicking, kite flying and fishing. Take bus 11 from the Broadway T station.

CHILDREN'S MUSEUM

☎ 617-426-6500; www.bostonchildrens museum.org; 300 Congress St; adult/ infant/senior & child $12/free/9, Fri evenings $1; 🕐 10am-5pm Sat-Thu, to 9pm Fri; 🚇 South Station; 🅿 ♿ ♿

After a major renovation and expansion, the Children's Museum is the best play date your kid will have all year. Who wouldn't want to play inside a bubble exhibit, on a two-story climbing maze, on a rock-climbing wall or with a hands-on construction site?

FORT POINT ARTS COMMUNITY

☎ 617-423-4299; www.fortpointarts .org; 300 Summer St; 🕐 9am-3:30pm Mon-Wed, to 10pm Thu & Fri, 5-10pm Sat; 🚇 South Station

FPAC is the heart and soul of this neighborhood. Since 1978, dozens of artists have lived and worked in this refurbished big-windowed warehouse. See the work of the talented collective in the on-site gallery.

ICA

☎ 617-478-3100; www.icaboston.org; 100 Northern Ave; adult/child/senior & student $12/free/10; 🕐 10am-5pm Tue, Wed, Sat & Sun, to 9pm Thu & Fri; 🚇 South Station; 🅿 ♿ ♿

The Institute of Contemporary Art is a work of art in itself – a striking

---

JFK IS OK

The legacy of JFK is ubiquitous in Boston, but the official memorial to the 35th president is the **John F Kennedy Library & Museum** (☎ 617-514-1600; www.jfklibrary.org; Columbia Point, Dorchester; adult/child/senior & student $12/9/10; 🕐 9am-5pm; 🚇 JFK/UMass; 🅿 ♿), housed in a striking, modern marble building designed by IM Pei. The museum is a fitting tribute to JFK's life and legacy. Videos re-create history for visitors who may or may not remember the early 1960s. The newest addition is an exhibit devoted to the 'poetry and power' of JFK's inaugural address. Take the red line to JFK/UMass and catch a free shuttle bus (departs every 20 minutes) to Columbia Point.

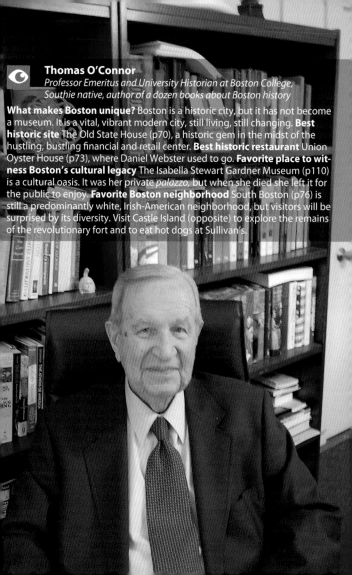

Thomas O'Connor
Professor Emeritus and University Historian at Boston College, Southie native, author of a dozen books about Boston history

What makes Boston unique? Boston is a historic city, but it has not become a museum. It is a vital, vibrant modern city, still living, still changing. **Best historic site** The Old State House (p70), a historic gem in the midst of the hustling, bustling financial and retail center. **Best historic restaurant** Union Oyster House (p73), where Daniel Webster used to go. **Favorite place to witness Boston's cultural legacy** The Isabella Stewart Gardner Museum (p110) is a cultural oasis. It was her private *palazzo*, but when she died she left it for the public to enjoy. **Favorite Boston neighborhood** South Boston (p76) is still a predominantly white, Irish-American neighborhood, but visitors will be surprised by its diversity. Visit Castle Island (opposite) to explore the remains of the revolutionary fort and to eat hot dogs at Sullivan's.

glass structure cantilevered over a waterside plaza. The spacious light-filled interior allows for multimedia presentations, educational programs and studio space. More importantly, it provides the venue for the development of the ICA's permanent collection of 21st-century art.

🍴 EAT

BARKING CRAB *Seafood* $$
☎ 617-426-2722; www.barkingcrab .com; 88 Sleeper St; 🕑 lunch & dinner; 🚇 South Station
Big buckets of crabs, steamers dripping in lemon and butter,

Get some crabs in your claws at the Barking Crab

paper plates piled high with all things fried… The food here is plentiful and cheap, and you eat it at communal picnic tables overlooking the water. Beer flows freely.

🍴 FLOUR *Bakery & Café* $
☎ 617-338-4333; www.flourbakery.com; 12 Farnsworth St; 🕑 7am-7pm Mon-Fri, 8am-6pm Sat, 9am-3pm Sun; 🚇 South Station; ♿
Flour implores patrons to 'make life sweeter…eat dessert first!' It's hard to resist at this pastry-lover's paradise. But be sure to save room for sandwiches, soups, salads and other fresh, delicious lunchtime fare.

🍴 SPORTELLO
Italian & Bakery $$
☎ 617-737-1234; www.sportelloboston .com; 348 Congress St; 🕑 breakfast, lunch & dinner; 🚇 South Station
Modern and minimalist, the latest brainchild of Barbara Lynch fits right into this up-and-coming urban 'hood. At the *sportello,* or lunch counter, suited yuppies indulge in sophisticated soups and salads and decadent polenta and pasta dishes.

🍴 YANKEE LOBSTER
FISH MARKET *Seafood* $$
☎ 617-345-9799; 300 Northern Ave; 🕑 10am-7pm Mon-Fri, to 8pm Sat, to 5pm Sun; 🚇 South Station

Longtime fisherfolk, the Zanti family recently opened this retail fish market, scattered with a few tables in case you want to dine in. And you do… Order something simple like fish and chips or a lobster roll, accompany it with a cold beer, and you will not be disappointed.

 # DRINK

DRINK *Cocktail Lounge*
☎ 617-695-1806; www.drinkfortpoint
.com; 348 Congress St S; 🕑 4pm-1am;
🚇 South Station

There is no cocktail menu at this old-time speakeasy. Instead you have a little chat with the bartender, and he or she will whip something up according to your specifications. They take the art of drink mixology seriously – and you will to, after you sample one of their concoctions!

FARRAGUT HOUSE *Irish Pub*
☎ 617-268-6348; www.farraguthouse
.com; 149 P St; 🚇 Broadway; Ⓟ 🚻
Stroll over from Castle Island to whet your whistle with a slowly

drawn Guinness. Owned by a real live Dubliner, this is a favorite Southie hangout, featuring live music from the old country.

LUCKY'S *Retro Bar*
☎ 617-357-5825; www.luckyslounge
.com; 355 Congress St S; 🕑 11am-2am
Sun-Fri, 6pm-2am Sat; 🚇 South Station

Step inside Lucky's and let your eyes adjust to a delightfully gritty lounge from another era. It's a brilliant stop for happy-hour cocktails, weekend dancing and Sinatra Sundays. PS There's no sign; just go inside.

 # PLAY

SOUTH BOSTON BEACHES
Outdoor Activities
Day Blvd, South Boston; 🕑 dawn-dusk;
🚇 Broadway; Ⓟ 🚻

West of Castle Island, 3 miles of beaches offer opportunities for swimming in an urban setting. L and M St beaches are adjacent to each other along Day Blvd while Carson Beach is further west.

>CHINATOWN & THEATER DISTRICT

These overlapping neighborhoods are home to Boston's lively theater scene, its most hip-hop-happening nightclubs and its best international dining. Ethnically and economically diverse, they border Boston's Downtown districts, but they are edgier and artier. Although it's only a few blocks wide, the Theater District has long served as a pre-Broadway staging area. Many landmark theaters have recently received facelifts, and their colorful marquees and posh patrons have revived the aura of 'bright lights, big city.'

Chinatown is overflowing with ethnic restaurants, live poultry and fresh produce markets, teahouses and textile shops. Newspaper boxes carry Mandarin and Cantonese publications, while phone booths are topped with pagodas. As well as the Chinese, this tight-knit community also includes Cambodians, Vietnamese and Laotians. Chinatown is a particularly popular dining destination for the postclubbing crowd, as many of these restaurants are open until all hours.

CHINATOWN & THEATER DISTRICT

👁 SEE
Chinatown
  Gate & Park 1 D2

🏠 SHOP
Calamus Bookstore 2 E2
Central China Book Co ... 3 D2
Cheng Kwong Market 4 D1

🍴 EAT
Apollo 5 D2
China Pearl 6 D2
Emperor's Garden 7 C2
Finale Desserterie 8 B2
Gourmet Dumpling
  House 9 D2

Jacob Wirth 10 C2
Jumbo Seafood 11 D2
Montien 12 C2
My Thai Vegan
  Café 13 C2
O Ya 14 E2
Peach Farm ....(see 16)
Shabu-Zen 15 D2
Suishaya 16 D2
Via Matta 17 A2
Xinh Xinh 18 C2

📺 DRINK
Corner Pub 19 E2
Intermission
  Tavern 20 C2
Troquet 21 B1

⭐ PLAY
Blue Man Group 22 B2
Boston Lyric
  Opera ....(see 28)
Citi Performing
  Arts Center 23 C2
Dick's Beantown
  Comedy Vault 24 C1
Estate 25 B1
Jacques Cabaret 26 B2
Opera Boston 27 C2
Shear Madness ....(see 22)
Shubert Theatre 28 C2
Wang Theatre ....(see 23)
Wilbur Theatre 29 C2

SEE

👁 CHINATOWN GATE & PARK

cnr Beach St & Surface Rd; 🚇 **Chinatown**
A gift from the city of Taipei, this decorative gate, or *paifong*, is the official entrance to Chinatown. Surrounding the gate and anchoring the southern end of the Rose Kennedy Greenway is Chinatown Park, which incorporates elements of feng shui into its design.

🛍 SHOP

📕 CALAMUS BOOKSTORE
Bookstore

☎ 617-338-1931; www.calamusbooks .com; 92 South St; 🚇 South Station
Inspired by Walt Whitman's *Calamus Poems*, Boston's biggest and best GLBT bookstore is also a community center, with a full calendar of author talks and art exhibitions.

📕 CENTRAL CHINA BOOK CO
Bookstore

☎ 617-426-0888; 31D Harrison Ave; 🚇 Chinatown
Tucked into a basement in the heart of Chinatown, this little bookstore carries fiction, reference and children's books, as well as CDs and DVDs. The impressive inventory (over 100,000 titles) is almost exclusively Chinese language products.

🛒 CHENG KWONG MARKET
Food & Drink

☎ 617-423-3749; www.super88.com; 73-79 Essex St; 🕐 8:30am-7pm; 🚇 Chinatown
A partner of Super 88 (the leading Asian supermarket chain in Boston), Cheng Kwong specializes in exotic vegetables, tropical fruits and live seafood. What is this funny-shaped fruit, anyway?

EAT

🍴 APOLLO *Korean* $$

☎ 617-423-3888; 84-86 Harrison Ave; 🕐 lunch Mon-Fri, 5pm-4am nightly; 🚇 Chinatown

COMBAT ZONE

In the second half of the 20th century, the administration attempted to concentrate the city's sleaze into a sort of red-light district along Washington St. Although prostitution was technically illegal, strippers and other ladies of the night (and their clients) descended on this neighborhood, which reporters dubbed the `Combat Zone.' Residents were generally poor immigrants who had little say in the matter.

Investment and development mean that the heyday of the Combat Zone has passed. But this ethnic enclave continues to be jeopardized -- not by peep shows and porn theaters but by skyrocketing rents.

NEIGHBORHOODS

CHINATOWN & THEATER DISTRICT

Buy the poetry of Boston's own Walt Whitman at Calamus Bookstore (opposite)

When the clubs close, hungry and hammered nightlifers head to this Japanese-Korean joint. Fire up the hibachi grill for Korean BBQ doused in a secret sauce or stick with tried-and-true *bi bim bop*.

ⅲ FINALE DESSERTERIE
Café $$
☎ 617-423-3184; www.finaledesserts .com; 1 Columbus Ave; ☽ lunch & din- ner; ⓡ Arlington; Ⓥ
Finale focuses on the sweet treats that are often an afterthought. Accompanied by coffee, tea or port, it's a delightful indulgence with a capital D.

ⅲ GOURMET DUMPLING
HOUSE *Chinese & Taiwanese* $
☎ 617-338-6223; 52 Beach St; ⓡ Chinatown; Ⓥ
Fresh, doughy and delicious dumplings are the raison d'être at GDH. There is actually a full menu

of Taiwanese goodness, but it might be against the law to come here without ordering the *xiao long bao* (soup dumplings).

ⅲ JACOB WIRTH *German* $$
☎ 617-338-8586; www.jacobwirth.com; 31-37 Stuart St; ☽ lunch & dinner; ⓡ Boylston; ♿
This atmospheric Bavarian beer hall is Boston's second-oldest eatery, featuring endless German schnitzels and wurst, as well as 30 different draft beers. On Friday night (open until 1am), Jake hosts a sing-along that rouses the haus.

ⅲ JUMBO SEAFOOD
Chinese & Seafood $$
☎ 617-542-2823; www.newjumbo seafoodrestaurant.com; 5 Hudson St; ☽ 11am-1am Sun-Thu, to 4am Fri & Sat; ⓡ Chinatown; Ⓥ
It says seafood on the sign. And it looks like seafood, judging by the

NEIGHBORHOODS

CHINATOWN & THEATER DISTRICT

It's well worth visiting Boston's second-oldest restaurant, Jacob Wirth (p85)

huge tanks of lobster, crabs and fish. But it's not only seafood on the menu, which represents the best of Hong Kong cuisine. Great lunch specials.

MONTIEN *Thai* $$
☎ 617-338-5600; www.montien-boston .com; 63 Stuart St; lunch & dinner Mon-Sat, dinner Sun; Boylston; V
There's nothing fancy going on at Montien, but Thai connoisseurs keep coming back time and time again for drunken noodles and pad thai. If you really know your stuff, ask for the authentic Thai menu.

MY THAI VEGAN CAFÉ
Thai $
☎ 617-451-2395; 3 Beach St; lunch & dinner; Chinatown; V
The name says it rather clearly. Thai (noodle soups, dumplings and pad thai). Vegan (animal-free

zone). As a café it's not the coziest place you'll ever eat, but the animals aren't complaining.

O YA *Japanese & Sushi* $$$
☎ 617-654-9900; www.oyarestaurant boston.com; 9 East St; dinner Tue-Sat; South Station; V
Oh yeah, O Ya. Boston's food community can't stop talking about this newcomer, which is winning all kinds of awards, not to mention plaudits from the *New York Times* food critic. Sushi with an unprecedented, out-of-this-world twist.

SHABU-ZEN *Japanese* $$
☎ 617-292-8828; www.shabuzen.com; 16 Tyler St; lunch & dinner daily, to midnight Thu-Sat; Chinatown
Shabu-shabu is fun to make and fun to eat. Choose from a variety of thinly sliced seafood and meats, a plate of fresh vegetables and an

array of homemade broths, then cook it up in a hot pot.

🍴 SUISHAYA *Korean & Sushi* $$
☎ 617-423-3848; 2 Tyler St;
🕙 11:30am-2am; 🚇 Chinatown
Suishaya serves reliably excellent food at any time of day, but it's even more delicious after midnight. We're pretty sure that has less to do with the food itself, and more to do with the patrons coming in from a night on the dance floor.

🍴 VIA MATTA *Italian* $$$
☎ 617-422-0008; www.viamattarestau rant.com; 79 Park Plaza; 🕙 11:30am-1am; 🚇 Arlington
Although there is a tasteful trendy dining room at Via Matta, it's more enticing to settle into the restaurant's dark, sexy *caffe*. The limited menu offers pizzas, bruschettas and other small plates late into the night.

🍴 XINH XINH
Vietnamese $$
☎ 617-422-0501; 7 Beach St; 🕙 lunch & dinner; 🚇 Chinatown;
On a cold day, nothing is more satisfying than a hot, hearty bowl of *pho*, the sometimes exotic, always fragrant and flavorful Vietnamese noodle soup.

🍸 DRINK

🍸 CORNER PUB *Dive Bar*
☎ 617-542-7080; 162 Lincoln St;
🚇 South Station
You have to ask yourself what you are looking for in a drinking establishment. If the answer is $3 beers

---

DIM SUM
Small plates are quite the rage in all realms of dining, so why not Chinese? Dim sum (meaning 'touch the heart') is a Cantonese cuisine that involves lots of light dishes, usually served with tea. It is a morning or midday meal, especially on weekends, holidays or other special occasions, a sort of Chinese brunch.

Dozens of dishes are offered, including dumplings, buns, rice-noodle rolls, spare ribs, stuffed lotus leafs and *congee* (rice porridge). There is also dessert, most typically and deliciously an egg tart. Everything is accompanied by tea.

Usually, there is no menu. Instead, staff push carts around the dining room and patrons can pick what they like. Here are some of our favorite places to dabble in dim sum:
China Pearl (☎ 617-426-4338; 9 Tyler St; 🕙 8:30am-11pm; 🚇 Chinatown)
Emperor's Garden (☎ 617-482-8898; 690 Washington St; 🕙 9am-9pm Sun-Thu, to 10pm Fri & Sat; 🚇 Chinatown)
Peach Farm (☎ 617-482-3332; 4 Tyler St; 🕙 11am-3am; 🚇 Chinatown)

NEIGHBORHOODS

CHINATOWN & THEATER DISTRICT

and a hard-core local clientele, then come to the Corner Pub. Bonus: new clean bathrooms.

INTERMISSION TAVERN
Pub

☎ 617-451-5997; www.intermission tavern.com; 228 Tremont St; 🚇 Boylston
The theater theme here is quaint, considering the central location on Tremont St. Masks of Comedy and Tragedy adorn the façade, while the interior is plastered with show posters, creating an ideal ambience for a drink after the show.

TROQUET *Wine Bar*

☎ 617-695-9463; www.troquetboston .com; 140 Boylston St; 🚇 Boylston
Nibble at French hors d'oeuvres while sipping complementary wines, selected to perfectly please your palette. This all takes place in a slick setting opposite the Boston Common.

PLAY

BLUE MAN GROUP
Performing Arts

☎ 617-931-2787; www.blueman.com; 74 Warrenton St; 🚇 Boylston
Blue Man Group is a troupe of entertainers who do clever and crazy things with paint, lights and acrobatics (but not talking). These men with blue faces have been

doing their thing at the Charles Playhouse for years.

BOSTON LYRIC OPERA *Opera*

☎ 617-542-6772; www.blo.org; 265 Tremont St (Shubert Theatre Box Office); tickets $33-112; 🚇 Boylston
The usual house of the BLO is the Shubert Theatre (part of the Citi Performing Arts Center), where you'll see *Don Giovanni*, *Rusalka* or *The Magic Flute*. Look out for special productions for families and children.

CITI PERFORMING ARTS CENTER *Performing Arts Venue*

☎ 617-482-9393; www.citicenter.org; 270 Tremont St; tickets $45-95; 🚇 Boylston
This artistic behemoth includes two different venues. The opulent and enormous Wang Theatre, built in 1925, has one of the largest stages in the country. Across the street, the more intimate Shubert Theatre is known as the 'Little Princess' of the Theater District. These theaters host all kinds of performances. from music and theater to comedy and dance.

DICK'S BEANTOWN COMEDY VAULT *Comedy*

☎ 800-401-2221; www.dickdoherty .com; 124 Boylston St; 🕑 shows 8:30pm Mon-Thu, 9pm Fri, 8pm & 10:15pm Sat, 9pm Sun; admission $12-20; 🚇 Boylston

Local funny guy Dick Doherty invites you into his subterranean space to laugh your head off, with him or with one of his regular helpers. The Comedy Vault is also the home of Joey DeVito, the R-rated hypnotist.

⭐ ESTATE *Dance Club*
☎ 617-351-7000; www.theestateboston
.com; 1 Boylston Pl; ⏱ Thu-Sat;
🚇 Boylston; 🅿
Thursdays are for gays and other 'glam' types. Fridays are for music mavens who want to see the biggest names in DJs. But whatever night you come, dress to impress the bouncer, who holds the key to your entry into this luxury lounge.

⭐ JACQUES CABARET
Gay Cabaret
☎ 617-426-8902; www.jacquescabaret
.com; 76 Broadway; ⏱ 11am-midnight
Mon-Sat, noon-midnight Sun;
🚇 Arlington
Are you curious about what went down around here before gentrification? Head to this holdover, an unexpected, out-of-the-way club with low-budget drag shows every night.

⭐ OPERA BOSTON *Opera*
☎ 617-451-3388; www.operaboston
.org; 219 Tremont St (Cutler Majestic Box Office); tickets $24-99; 🚇 Boylston

This acclaimed opera company is known for performing rarely heard works of masters, as well as an experimental repertoire of more recent vintage. Opera Boston plays out of the gilded Cutler Majestic Theater.

⭐ SHEAR MADNESS *Comedy*
☎ 617-426-5255; www.shearmadness
.com; 74 Warrenton Ave; admission $42;
🚇 Boylston
If you like audience participation, you might enjoy Shear Madness, America's longest-running comedy. It's shear madness because it's set in a hair salon and the half-play, half-improvisational plotline is, well, mad. See it go down at the Charles Playhouse.

⭐ WILBUR THEATRE *Comedy*
☎ 617-931-2000; www.thewilbur
theatre.com; 246 Tremont St; tickets
$10-40; 🚇 Boylston; 🅿
The Wilbur Theatre was recently acquired by the Comedy Connection, Boston's best-known and longest-running comedy club. This means that the Wilbur is now a comedy theater – apparently the first theater in the country dedicated to tickling your funny bone. This is where you can most reliably find big-name acts. Parking costs $10.

>BACK BAY

Boston's most genteel residential and retail neighborhood, Back Bay's grand boulevards are lined with majestic brownstones, while fashionable Newbury St is replete with boutiques and cafés.

But there is a reason why it's called the Back Bay. Indeed, up until the 1850s, this was a marshy tidal flat that drained from the Charles River.

The city's growth in the 19th century spurred the plan to fill in the Back Bay and create a new neighborhood, complete with Parisian boulevards and glorious green parks. Commonwealth Ave was lined with brownstones and dotted with public art. Copley Sq was graced with architectural masterpieces such as the Renaissance Revival Boston Public Library (p92) and the Richardsonian Trinity Church (p93). And to the great relief of future visitors, the city created an orderly grid of streets with names in alphabetical order (a remarkable contrast to the rest of the city).

BACK BAY

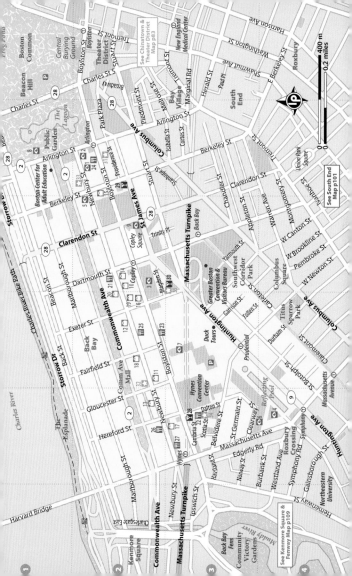

SEE

◎ BOSTON PUBLIC LIBRARY

☎ 617-536-5400; www.bpl.org; 700 Boylston St; admission free; ⏰ 9am-9pm Mon-Thu, to 5pm Fri & Sat year-round, 1-5pm Sun Oct-May; 🚇 Copley

The old McKim building of the BPL is notable for its magnificent façade and exquisite interior art, not to mention its untold treasures in special collections. Pick up a free brochure and take a self-guided tour; alternatively, free guided tours depart from the entrance hall.

◎ CHRISTIAN SCIENCE CHURCH

☎ 617-450-3790; www.tfccs.com; 175 Huntington Ave; admission free; ⏰ noon-4pm Tue, 1-4pm Wed, noon-5pm Thu-Sat, 11am-3pm Sun, service 10am Sun; 🚇 Symphony; ♿

Known as the 'Mother Church,' this is the international home base for the Church of Christ, Scientist (Christian Science), founded by Mary Baker Eddy in 1866. Tour the grand classical revival basilica, which can seat 3000 worshippers, listen to the 14,000-pipe organ and linger on the expansive plaza with its 670ft-long reflecting pool.

◎ MAPPARIUM

☎ 617-450-7000, 888-222-3711; www.marybakereddylibrary.org; adult/child, senior & student $6/4; ⏰ 10am-4pm Tue-Sun; 🚇 Symphony; ♿ 👶

Inside the Mary Baker Eddy Library, the Mapparium is a room-size, stained-glass globe that visitors walk through on a glass bridge. The acoustics, which surprised even the designer, allow everyone in the room to hear even the tiniest whisper.

◎ PRUDENTIAL CENTER SKYWALK

☎ 617-859-0648; www.prudentialcenter.com; adult/child/senior & student $12/8/10; ⏰ 10am-10pm Mar-Oct, to 8pm Nov-Feb; 🚇 Prudential; Ⓟ ♿ 👶

GALLERY HOPPING ON NEWBURY STREET

While much of the art action has moved south, Newbury St is still home to some high-fallutin' galleries, especially at the end near the Public Garden. Here are a few of our favorites:

Alpha Gallery (☎ 617-536-4465; www.alphagallery.com; 38 Newbury St; ⏰ 10am-5:30pm Tue-Sat, 11am-5:30pm Sun; 🚇 Arlington)

Barbara Krakow Gallery (☎ 617-262-4490; www.barbarakrakowgallery.com; 10 Newbury St; ⏰ 10am-5:30pm Tue-Sat; 🚇 Arlington)

Gallery NAGA (☎ 617-267-9060; www.gallerynaga.com; 67 Newbury St; ⏰ 10am-5:30pm Tue-Sat; 🚇 Arlington)

Boston's second-tallest building provides a bird's-eye view of the city from its 50th-floor Skywalk. Completely enclosed by glass, the skywalk offers spectacular 360° views of Boston and Cambridge, accompanied by an entertaining audio tour (with a special version catering to kids).

PUBLIC GARDEN

The Public Garden is a 24-acre botanical oasis of Victorian flower-beds, verdant grass, and weeping willows trees shading a tranquil lagoon. Taking a ride on the **Swan Boats** (☎ 617-522-1966; www.swan boats.com; adult/child/senior $2.75/1.25/2; ⏰ 10am-4pm mid-Apr–mid-Sep; 👶) in the lagoon has been a Boston tradition since 1877.

TRINITY CHURCH

☎ **617-536-0944; www.trinity churchboston.org; 206 Clarendon St; adult/child/senior & student $6/free/4; ⏰ 10am-3:30pm Mon-Fri, 9am-4pm Sat, 1-5pm Sun; 🚇 Copley; ♿**

Trinity Church is the ultimate example of Richardsonian Roman-esque architecture. The interior is an awe-inspiring array of murals and stained glass, most by artist John La Farge. The jeweled window *Christ in Majesty* is considered one of America's finest examples of stained-glass art. Free architectural tours are offered following Sunday service at 11:15am.

Department store Louis Boston (p95)

🛍 SHOP

🏬 CLOSET, INC
Secondhand Clothing

☎ **617-536-1919; www.closetboston .com; 175 Newbury St; 🚇 Copley**

The name is apropos, as it really does feel like some fashion maven's overstuffed closet. Big names without the big price tags, this is a boutique full of second-hand designer clothes.

NEIGHBORHOODS

BACK BAY

ENVI *Women's Clothing*
☎ 617-267-3684; www.shopenvi.com;
164 Newbury St; ⏱ 11am-8pm Mon-Sat,
noon-6pm Sun; ⛎ Copley
You think you look good in green?
Envi's collection of eco-conscious
clothing focuses on organic and
recycled materials, sustainably
produced and fairly traded.

FAIRY SHOP *Gift Shop*
☎ 617-262-2520; www.thefairyshop
.com; 272 Newbury St; ⛎ Hynes
'Chillin' with my gnomies' reads the
T-shirt that is the top-selling item
at this quirky store. It also carries
fairies – yes, like Tinker Bell – in all
shapes and sizes, as well as crystals,
comic books and magic potions.

Jake's House makes you feel good about life

HEMPEST
Clothing & Home Accessories
☎ 617-421-9944; www.hempest.com;
207 Newbury St; ⏱ 11am-8pm Mon-Sat,
noon-6pm Sun; ⛎ Copley
Cannabis...it's not just for smoking
anymore. Indeed, *Cannabis sativa*
(commonly called hemp) is used
for making clothing, furniture,
soaps and lotions. Hemp is a
rapidly renewable and versatile
resource that is economically and
environmentally beneficial…if only
it were legal to grow in the US.

JAKE'S HOUSE
Sportswear & T-shirts
☎ 617-262-5068; www.lifeisgood.com;
285 Newbury St; ⛎ Copley
Jake will surely make you smile.
T-shirts and baseball caps depict
him engaged in guitar playing,
dog walking, coffee drinking,
mountain climbing and just about
every other good-vibe diversion
you might enjoy.

KARMALOOP
Clothing & Streetwear
☎ 617-369-0100; www.karmaloop.com
/boston; 160 Newbury St; ⏱ 10am-8pm
Mon-Thu, to 9pm Fri & Sat, 11am-7pm
Sun; ⛎ Copley
You know you're bad. Get yourself
into Karmaloop for some tough-
looking printed Ts or some jeans
that hang off your hips or some hip-
hop-happening colorful sneakers.

◪ LOUIS BOSTON
Department Store

☎ 617-262-6100; www.louisboston
.com; 234 Berkeley St; ⏲ 11am-6pm
Mon, 10am-6pm Tue & Wed, 10am-7pm
Thu-Sat; ⓡ Arlington

Louis Boston (pronounced 'loo-eez' please) is four stories of ultra-trendy clothing and cool, contemporary house wares in a beautiful Back Bay town house. At the time of press, Louis Boston was searching for a new location. Check its website for updates.

◪ MARATHON SPORTS
Sportswear

☎ 617-267-4774; www.marathonsports
.com; 671 Boylston St; ⏲ 10:30am-
7:30pm Mon-Fri, 10am-6pm Sat, noon-
6pm Sun; ⓡ Copley

A sports store for runners. Staff members know their shoes, and they also know that their store offers the perfect view of the Boston Marathon finish line.

◪ NEWBURY COMICS
Music

☎ 617-236-4930; www.newburycomics
.com; 332 Newbury St; ⓡ Hynes

Although Newbury Comics carries a lot of silly stuff including 'Peace Love Vampires' T-shirts and Barack Obama action figures, this place is really all about the music. It's Boston's best place to buy cheap CDs and DVDs.

◪ OAK
Clothing, Jewelry & Accessories

☎ 617-421-9944; www.oakboston.com;
245 Newbury St; ⏲ 11am-7pm Mon &
Wed-Sat, noon-6pm Sun; ⓡ Copley

Who doesn't need a hand-knitted iPod case? Or Lego cufflinks? Or floral undies made out of repurposed fabrics? All of the stuff at Oak is handmade by local artisans, guaranteeing you a cute and clever souvenir.

◪ SECOND TIME AROUND
Secondhand Clothing

☎ 617-247-3504; 176 Newbury St;
⏲ 10am-8pm Mon-Sat, noon-6pm Sun;
ⓡ Copley

Come early and come often, because you never know what you're going to find; but you can be sure it will have a designer label. The secondhand clothing here includes a great selection of denim.

◪ SOCIETY OF ARTS &
CRAFTS *Arts & Crafts*

☎ 617-266-1810; www.societyofcrafts
.org; 175 Newbury St; ⏲ 10am-6pm
Mon-Sat, noon-5pm Sun; ⓡ Copley

This cooperative has been exhibiting the wares of local artists for over a century. Downstairs is retail space for creative handicrafts, while the upstairs gallery exhibits emerging and established artists.

John Jacobs
Co-founder of Life is Good, designer of T-shirts and baseball caps, spreader of good vibes

How does Boston reflect the 'Life is Good' mentality? Bostonians don't have an overblown sense of themselves – humor and humility are key for LIG. LIG is about appreciating what you have and celebrating life's simple pleasures, and Boston is good at celebrating (ever since that Tea Party). **Best reminder that life is good** Playing Frisbee on the Esplanade (p99), playing wiffleball on the Common (p58), kayaking on the Charles (p65). **Best place to recuperate or celebrate afterwards** Sevens Ale House (p65), Other Side Cosmic Café (p111), Sonsie (p98), Vault (p74) **Best time to be in Boston** Come in June for the Life is Good Festival (p28), one day of old-school summer fun and a killer lineup of live music. **Best way to spread good vibes** Donate to Project Joy (www.projectjoy.com), a local nonprofit that provides play therapy for kids that have been through trauma.

🍴 EAT

🍴 BOUCHÉE French $$$

☎ 617-450-4343; www.bouchee
brasserie.com; 159 Newbury St; 🕑 lunch
& dinner; 🚇 Copley

This 'urban brasserie' in the heart
of Newbury St offers a perfect pit
stop after a day of shopping and
strolling. At the 1st-floor wine bar,
a full-bodied red and a bowl of
French onion soup warm the body
and the soul.

🍴 JASPER WHITE'S SUMMER SHACK Seafood $$

☎ 617-867-9955; www.summer
shackrestaurant.com; 50 Dalton St;
🕑 11am-11pm Sun-Thu, to 1am Fri &
Sat; 🚇 Hynes

Portions are large and prepa-
rations are straightforward:
specialties include traditional
lobster rolls, steamed clams and a
magnificently huge raw bar.

🍴 L'ESPALIER French $$$

☎ 617-262-3023; www.lespalier.com;
774 Boylston St; 🕑 dinner Mon-Sat;
🚇 Prudential

Despite its move in 2008,
L'Espalier remains the crème de la
crème of Boston's culinary scene.
The tasting menus change daily,
but usually include a degustation of caviar, a degustation of
seasonal vegetables and recommended wine pairings.

🍴 PARISH CAFÉ & BAR
Sandwiches $

☎ 617-247-4777; www.parishcafe
.com; 361 Boylston St; 🕑 noon-2am;
🚇 Arlington; Ⓥ

Sample the creations from some of
Boston's most famous chefs (Lydia
Shire, Ken Oringer and Barbara
Lynch) without exhausting your
expense account. The rotating ros-
ter presents salads and sandwiches
designed by these local celebrities.

🍴 PIATTINI
Italian, Small Plates & Wine Bar $$

☎ 617-536-2020; www.piattini.com;
226 Newbury St; 🕑 lunch & dinner Mon-
Fri, dinner Sat & Sun; 🚇 Copley; Ⓥ

This intimate enoteca (wine bar)
is a delightful setting to sample
the flavors of Italy. The menu of

EAT YOUR WORDS

When it comes to food and drink, some-
times Bostonians have a funny way of
expressing themselves. Here's your
food-wise phrase book:
> Bubbler – water fountain
> Frappe – milkshake
> Grinder – a heated submarine
  sandwich
> Jimmies – chocolate sprinkles (on
  ice cream)
> Order – groceries
> Packie – liquor store
> Scrod – white-fish catch of the day
> Steamers – steamed clams
> Tonic – carbonated soft drink; soda

NEIGHBORHOODS

BACK BAY

piattini, or 'small plates,' means you don't have to choose just one! Wines by the glass are accompanied by tasting notes and fun facts.

SONSIE International $$$

☎ 617-351-2500; www.sonsieboston.com; 327 Newbury St; 🕑 breakfast, lunch & dinner; 🚇 Hynes

This trendy spot continues to attract devotees with its interesting, eclectic menu, not to mention the eye candy that patronizes the place. Tiny, café-style tables are crammed into the front of the restaurant, offering a fabulous view onto Newbury St.

TRIDENT BOOKSELLERS & CAFÉ International $$

☎ 617-267-8688; www.tridentbookscafe.com; 338 Newbury St; 🕑 9am-midnight; 🚇 Hynes; Ⓥ

Is Trident a bookstore with an amazingly eclectic menu or a café with a super selection of reading material? It doesn't really matter, so long as you find something to browse while you munch on lunch.

DRINK

BUKOWSKI TAVERN Dive Bar

☎ 617-437-9999; 50 Dalton St; 🚇 Hynes

Yes, you got the right address. This tough-love favorite is indeed located inside a parking garage. What a perfect place to sample more than 100 kinds of beer (well, some of them anyway). Cash only.

COTTONWOOD CAFÉ Tex-Mex Bar

☎ 617-247-2225; www.cottonwoodboston.com; 222 Berkeley St; 🚇 Copley

Cottonwood constantly wins acclaim for its excellent margaritas. There are 10 different versions, served by the glass or by the pitcher, which should keep you busy for a while.

MINIBAR Cocktail Lounge

☎ 617-424-8500; www.minibarboston.com; 51 Huntington Ave; 🚇 Copley

Those guests who were getting lonely drinking in their rooms at the Copley Square Hotel can now raid the minibar downstairs. It's a swank space with cushy couches, sexy people and good vibes.

⭐ PLAY

⭐ BACK BAY YOGA STUDIO Health & Fitness

☎ 617-375-0785; www.backbayyoga.com; 364 Boylston St; per class $15; 🕑 6am-9pm Mon-Thu, to 7pm Fri, 9:30am-5:30pm Sat, 8am-6:30pm Sun; 🚇 Arlington

Services from massage to meditation, as well as all forms of yoga.

Four to nine classes are offered daily.

⭐ EMERGE BY GIULIANO
Health & Fitness

☎ 617-437-0006; www.emergespa
salon.com; 275 Newbury St; 🚇 Hynes
Giuliano tempts both men and women. The mahogany Men's Club offers not only a shave and a haircut, but also manicures, pedicures, waxing and massage. Plus there's a whole host of treatments (mostly massage) for couples.

DOWN BY THE RIVER, DOWN BY THE BANKS OF THE RIVER CHARLES

The southern bank of the Charles River Basin is an enticing urban escape, with grassy knolls and cooling waterways, all designed by Frederick Law Olmsted. The **Charles River Esplanade** (www.es planadeassociation.org) is dotted with public art, including an oversized bust of Arthur Fiedler, long-time conductor of the Boston Pops. Paths along the river are ideal for cycling, jogging or walking. The Esplanade stretches almost 3 miles along the Boston shore of the Charles River, from the Museum of Science to BU Bridge.

⭐ G SPA *Health & Fitness*

☎ 617-267-4772; www.gspa.com;
35 Newbury St; 🚇 Arlington
'Quickie' treatments provide a quick pick-me-up in 25 minutes or less. These speedy treaties save you time and money, as they are priced $45 and under. Splurge options also available.

⭐ KINGS *Bowling*

☎ 617-266-2695; www.kingsbackbay
.com; 50 Dalton St; game/shoe rental
$8/$5; 🕑 5pm-2am Mon, 11:30-2am
Tue-Sun; 🚇 Hynes; 🅿
High-tech meets tenpin. Lined with neon and blinking with trippy graphics, Kings' lanes make you feel like you're bowling into the future.

⭐ SAINT *Nightclub*

☎ 617-236-1134; www.saintboston
.com; 90 Exeter St; 🚇 Copley; 🅿
This 'boutique nitery' is more intimate than your typical nightclub, with two basement-level rooms: a white marbly dance room and a crimson-colored lounge with carpet on the ceiling (heaven and hell, perhaps?) Reserve online or arrive right at 10pm to ensure you get in.

>SOUTH END

What better fate to befall a neighborhood than to attract the attention of the gay community? This once-rough area has been transformed by Boston's queer eye, and now it is the city's hottest spot for yuppies of all sexual orientations.

The South End boasts the country's largest concentration of Victorian row houses, lining lovely streets including elliptical Union Park and intimate Rutland Sq. Now the neighborhood is also bursting with Boston's trendiest restaurants, bars and boutiques. Artists are pushing out the edges, converting the old warehouses into studio and gallery space and creating a new art district, dubbed 'SoWa.'

The South End is certainly the city's most diverse neighborhood, both ethnically and economically, and there are still housing projects and homeless shelters mixed in with the swanky stuff, adding to the rich mix. Keep your wits about you, and avoid going too far west of Mass Ave, especially at night.

SOUTH END

SEE

The South End may not be packed with historic sites or educational museums, but it is home to Boston's most dynamic art scene. Head to SoWa (the area south of Washington St) where there is a cluster of galleries along Thayer St and Harrison Ave, or to the Boston Center for the Arts (p107). These venues host an open studios event on the first Friday of every month from May to October (see p30).

SHOP

AUNT SADIE'S CANDLESTIX
Gift Shop
☎ 617-357-7117; www.auntsadiesinc
.com; 18 Union Park St; 🚇 Back Bay
If it smells nice, chances are you can buy it at Aunt Sadie's. Put the aromatherapy to work for you with bubble bath, smelly soaps, scented sachets or the name-sake candles. Scents range from fragrant to funky.

BOBBY FROM BOSTON
Vintage Clothing
☎ 617-423-9299; 19 Thayer St;
🕑 noon-6pm Mon-Sat; 🚇 Back Bay
Smoking jackets, bow ties, bomber jackets and more. Men from all over the greater Boston area come to the South End to peruse Bobby's amazing selection of classic

SOUTHWEST CORRIDOR PARK
The Southwest Corridor is a beautiful paved and landscaped walkway, running for 5 miles between Columbus and Huntington Aves. Leading from Back Bay through the South End to Jamaica Plain, it's an ideal place to walk, jog, bike or skate. Take the orange line to any stop between the Back Bay and Forest Hills stations.

clothing from another era. There is a smaller selection of women's wear, too.

MOTLEY
Vintage Clothing & Gifts
☎ 617-247-6969; www.shopmotley
.com; 623 Tremont St; 🚇 Back Bay
True enough, you probably don't need any of the items that this little shoebox of a store has to offer. But who can resist the comfy, clever T-shirts and true-blue vintage sports gear? The changing array of gift items is a gas, so it's a fun place to browse.

PARLOR
Women's Clothing
☎ 617-521-9005; www.shopparlor.com;
1248 Washington St; 🚇 New England Medical Center
Love the designer duds but can't stand the snooty 'tude in urban boutiques? Parlor defies that

description, specializing in friendly fashion advice to complement the upscale styles. Alluring outfits feature designers from New York and Los Angeles.

SOUTH END OPEN MARKET
Arts & Crafts

☎ 617-481-2257; www.southend openmarket.com; 540 Harrison Ave; ⏰ 10am-4pm Sun May-Oct; 🚇 New England Medical Center

Part flea market and part artists' market, this weekly outdoor event attracts over 100 vendors selling arts and crafts, as well as edgier art, vintage clothing, jewelry, local farm produce and homemade sweets. For antiques, go directly to the **SoWa Antiques Market** (☎ 617-862-4039; www.sowa antiquesmarket.com) inside the old trolley barn.

TURTLE
Women's Clothing

☎ 617-266-2610; www.turtleboston .com; 619 Tremont St; ⏰ 11am-7pm Tue-Fri, 10am-6pm Sat, noon-5pm Sun; 🚇 Back Bay

It's hard to say if Turtle is a fashion boutique or an art gallery. Edgy and innovative, this clothing shop focuses on emerging designers from around the world. You might want to hang your new sweater on the wall. This stuff is expensive (it's original art,

after all) so look for the sidewalk sales.

UNIFORM *Men's Clothing*

☎ 617-247-2360; www.uniformboston .com; 511 Tremont St; 🚇 Back Bay

Gentlemen, you are now in the South End, so there is no shame in being your fabulous fashion-forward self. Uniform caters to all the metrosexuals in this hipster 'hood, with cool, casual styles in clothing and accessories. Get your man purse here.

🍴 EAT

🍴 B&G OYSTERS
Seafood $$$

☎ 617-423-0550; www.bandgoysters .com; 550 Tremont St; ⏰ lunch & dinner; 🚇 Back Bay

Tiny and trendy, B&G is a sweet little spot to sip wine and slurp the freshest oysters from local waters.

🍴 DOUZO *Sushi* $$

☎ 617-859-8886; www.douzosushi.com; 131 Dartmouth St; ⏰ lunch & dinner; 🚇 Back Bay

Good-looking, smooth-talking urbanites come to Douzo to feast on raw fish, sip fancy cocktails and check each other out. It's usually a pretty pleasant experience, on all three counts.

Mike's City Diner satisfies the bacon-and-egg needs of Southies

🍴 FRANKLIN CAFÉ

American $$

☎ 617-350-0010; www.franklincafe
.com; 278 Shawmut Ave; ⏰ 5:30pm-
1:30am; 🚇 Back Bay; Ⓥ

Franklin was one of the first restau-
rants to cater to the beautiful boys
in the 'hood with New American
comfort food and a dynamic bar
scene. It's still a neighborhood
favorite with a trendy friendly vibe.

🍴 GASLIGHT, BRASSERIE DU

COIN *French* $$

☎ 617-422-0224; www.gaslight560.com;
560 Harrison Ave; ⏰ dinner Mon-Fri,
brunch & dinner Sat & Sun; 🚇 Back Bay

Dark and romantic, Gaslight is
an unpretentious and inviting
'brasserie on the corner,' offering
classic French fare and an excellent
selection of wines by the glass.

🍴 MIKE'S CITY DINER *Diner* $

☎ 617-267-9393; www.mikescitydiner
.com; 1714 Washington St; ⏰ breakfast
& lunch; 🚇 Massachusetts Ave

Mike knows that breakfast is the
most important meal of the day,
so he's serving up eggs and bacon
and bottomless cups of coffee.
Lunch is equally hearty, especially
when eaten at the counter. Cash
only.

🍴 MYERS & CHANG

Asian & Small Plates $$

☎ 617-542-5200; www.myersand
chang.com; 1145 Washington St;
⏰ lunch & dinner; 🚇 New England
Medical Center; Ⓥ

These two innovators have
created quite a stir with their
super-hip Asian fusion café. Fea-
turing delicious dumplings, spicy

stir-fries and oodles of noodles, the tapas-style menu means you can sample them all.

PICCO *Pizzeria* $$
☎ 617-927-0066; www.piccorestaurant .com; 513 Tremont St; 🕐 lunch & dinner; 🚇 Back Bay; 💻 Ⓥ ♿

Crispy thin crusts and interesting, even exotic, toppings make Picco the perennial favorite pizzeria in the South End. Delectable home-made ice cream doesn't hurt either.

SOUTH END BUTTERY
Bakery & Café $
☎ 617-482-1015; www.southendbut tery.com; 314 Shawmut Ave; 🕐 break-fast, lunch & dinner; 🚇 Back Bay

This button-sized bakery has been seducing South Enders with sinfully delicious cupcakes and pastries for several years. Now,

simple, seasonal dinner dishes are added to the delightful mix.

TORO *Spanish & Tapas* $$
☎ 617-536-4300; www.toro-restaurant .com; 1704 Washington St; 🕐 lunch & dinner Mon-Sat, brunch & dinner Sun; 🚇 Massachusetts Ave

Bursting with Spanish spirit, Toro is unique for its simple but sublime tapas. Free-flowing sangria and communal seating at butcher-block tables add to the lively atmosphere.

UNION BAR & GRILLE
American $$
☎ 617-423-0555; www.unionrestaurant .com; 1357 Washington St; 🕐 dinner Mon-Fri, brunch & dinner Sat & Sun; 🚇 Back Bay

Once an empty warehouse, Union is now an ever-popular

FOODIE SHOPS

South Enders like to eat. That's clear from the abundance of eateries that pack these streets. But they also like to cook, so this neighborhood features a few fancy food stores, too. Get your smelly cheeses, exotic spices and other unheard-of ingredients here.

Butcher Shop (☎ 617-423-4800; www.thebutchershopboston.com; 552 Tremont St; 🕐 lunch & dinner; 🚇 Back Bay) Cases filled with tantalizing cuts of meat, fresh foie gras and homemade sausages. If you can't wait, there's also a restaurant on site.

Plum Produce (☎ 617-423-7586; www.plumproduce.com; 106 Waltham St; 🕐 noon-8pm Mon-Sat, to 5pm Sun; 🚇 Back Bay) Fresh seasonal produce from Barbara Lynch's favorite local farms.

South End Formaggio (☎ 617-350-6996; www.southendformaggio.com; 268 Shawmut Ave; 🕐 9am-8pm Mon-Fri, to 7pm Sat, 11am-5pm Sun; 🚇 Back Bay) Olive oils, wines and dry goods. And cheese, oh, the cheese!

bar and grill that retains an industrial edge. The atmosphere is comfortable and convivial, and nobody balks at the excellent, affordable menu. Five-dollar cocktails mean you can have more than one!

☗ DRINK

☗ 28 DEGREES *Cocktail Lounge*
☎ 617-728-0728; www.28degrees
-boston.com; 1 Appleton St;
🕒 5pm-midnight; 🚇 Back Bay
'Over 40,883 Bellinis served,' boasts this super-slick cocktail bar. The cocktail of champagne, peach puree and vodka is just one on the list of perfectly chilled treats, which change seasonally.

☗ DELUX CAFÉ & LOUNGE
Dive Bar
☎ 617-338-5258; 100 Chandler St;
🕒 5pm-1am Mon-Sat; 🚇 Back Bay
Boston's favorite laid-back hipster bar, this divey place is tucked into an undistinguished corner of the South End. You can't beat the cramped quarters, Christmas lights and cartoons on the big screen. Hungry people should order the grilled-cheese sandwich.

☗ FLASH'S COCKTAILS
Cocktail Lounge
☎ 617-574-8888; www.flashscocktails
.com; 312 Stuart St; 🚇 Arlington; 🖵

'Flashback' with a classic martini or Manhattan, or 'flash-forward' with a modern invention such as a Dreamy-tini or a Winter Cosmo. Either way you'll love the retro atmo and the old-fashioned neon sign.

☗ FRITZ *Gay Sports Bar*
☎ 617-482-4428; www.fritzboston.com;
26 Chandler St; 🚇 Arlington
It's a little bit kitschy, it's a little bit rock and roll. Which is perfect for South End sports fans, who want to watch the Red Sox, but who prefer their TV screens enhanced by pink lights.

☗ MASA *Tex-Mex Bar*
☎ 617-338-8884; www.masarestaurant
.com; 439 Tremont St; 🚇 Back Bay or
Arlington
The huge draw here is happy hour, when tiny tapas – $1 each – fly off the menu and into your mouth. But Masa is also *magnífico* for Sunday brunch and Thursday night salsa dancing.

★ PLAY

★ BEEHIVE *Jazz Club*
☎ 617-423-0069; www.beehiveboston
.com; 541 Tremont St; admission free;
🕒 5pm-2am; 🚇 Copley
Housed in the basement of the Boston Center for the Arts, the Beehive has generated a lot of buzz. It's a retro repro of a Paris jazz club, complete with exposed brick walls,

Get jazzy with it at Wally's Café

intimate stage and hipster vibe. There's music every night, but it often takes a backseat to the scene.

⭐ **BOSTON CENTER FOR THE ARTS** *Theater*
☎ 617-933-8600; www.bcaonline.org; 539 Tremont St; 🚇 Back Bay
The centerpiece of the South End is this arts complex, housing gallery, performance and exhibition spaces. Some 20 small theater companies live here, producing Boston's most cutting-edge performances.

⭐ **CLUB CAFÉ** *Gay Club*
☎ 617-536-0966; www.clubcafe .com; 209 Columbus Ave; 🕐 Wed-Sat; 🚇 Arlington

Here is your glossy gay dance club, with plenty of beautiful bartenders plying their patrons with drinks, and carefully coiffed super studs dancing to Madonna remixes.

⭐ **WALLY'S CAFÉ** *Jazz Club*
☎ 617-424-1408; http://wallyscafe.com; 427 Massachusetts Ave; 🕐 11am-2am Mon-Sat, noon-2am Sun; 🚇 Massachusetts Ave
This old-school institution is the opposite of the Beehive, meaning it's gritty and small. And it's all about the music. Berklee students love this place, especially the weekend afternoon jam sessions.

>KENMORE SQUARE & FENWAY

You'll know you're in Kenmore Sq when you spot the landmark Citgo sign. This oddly beloved blinking billboard reminds Bostonians about baseball (home-run target), the marathon (25-mile marker) and everything they love about their city.

Kenmore Sq and Fenway are the epicenter of student life in Boston. In addition to the Boston University behemoth, which stretches along Commonwealth Ave, there are more than a half-dozen colleges in the area. As such, this neighborhood has a disproportionate share of clubs, inexpensive eateries and dormitories disguised as brownstones.

Fenway is a residential neighborhood south of the square. But Fenway takes on multiple meanings in Boston. It also refers to the Back Bay Fens, a tranquil and interconnected park system that's an integral link in the Emerald Necklace (see p113). Most importantly, of course, Fenway Park is where the Boston Red Sox play ball.

KENMORE SQUARE & FENWAY

◉ SEE
Isabella Stewart
   Gardner Museum 1 C4
Museum of Fine Arts 2 D3

▥ EAT
Audubon Circle 3 C2
Eastern Standard 4 D1
La Verdad 5 D2
Other Side Cosmic Café ...6 E2
Uburger 7 D1

▼ DRINK
Bleacher Bar 8 C2
Cask 'n Flagon 9 C2
Lower Depths 10 D1

★ PLAY
Boston Pops ....(see 11)
Boston Symphony
   Orchestra 11 E3
Church 12 C3
Fenway Park 13 D2

House of Blues 14 D2
Huntington Theatre
   Company 15 E3
Jillian's Billiard Club &
   Lucky Strike Lanes 16 D2

👁 SEE

👁 ISABELLA STEWART GARDNER MUSEUM

☎ 617-566-1401; www.gardnermu
seum.org; 280 The Fenway; adult/child/
student/senior $12/free/5/10; 🕑 11am-
5pm Tue-Sun; 🚇 Museum; ♿

The Venetian-style palazzo is a
monument to one woman's exquisite taste in art. 'Mrs Jack' Gardner's collection comprises 2000
priceless objects, including Italian
Renaissance and 17th-century
Dutch paintings. Free admission if
your name is Isabella.

👁 MUSEUM OF FINE ARTS

☎ 617-267-9300; www.mfa.org; 465
Huntington Ave; adult/child/senior &
student $17/6.50/15; 🕑 10am-5pm
Thu-Tue, to 10pm Wed; 🚇 Museum;
🅿 ♿ 🚻

The magnificent Museum of Fine
Arts is only getting better, as it
expands its exhibition space for
contemporary art and improves its
facilities for conservation. The museum's highlights are undoubtedly
its collection of American painting
and decorative arts (expected to
open in a new wing in 2010), as
well as its incredible collection of
French Impressionists. The West
Wing is open until 10pm on Thursdays and Fridays.

🍴 EAT

🍴 AUDUBON CIRCLE Pub $$

☎ 617-421-1910; www.auduboncircle
.us; 838 Beacon St; 🕑 11:30am-1am;
🚇 St Mary's

Not many people know that the
intersection of Beacon St and Park
Dr is called Audubon Circle (as
evidenced by the birds perching
on the light posts). But everyone
knows the eponymous pub,
popular for good food and good
vibes.

🍴 EASTERN STANDARD
American & French $$$

☎ 617-532-9100; www.easternstand
ard.com; 528 Commonwealth Ave;
🕑 lunch & dinner Mon-Fri, brunch &
dinner Sat & Sun; 🚇 Kenmore

WORTH THE TRIP: BROOKLINE

The John F Kennedy National Historic Site (☎ 617-566-7937; www.nps.gov/jofi; 83
Beals St; adult/child $3/free; 🕑 10am-4:30pm Wed-Sun May-Oct; 🚇 Coolidge Corner) oc-
cupies the modest three-story house that was JFK's birthplace and boyhood home. Matriarch
Rose Kennedy oversaw its restoration and furnishing in the late 1960s; today her narrative
sheds light on the Kennedy's family life. Take the green 'C' line to Coolidge Corner and walk
north on Harvard St.

The Koch Gallery in the Museum of Fine Arts (opposite)

It's hard to resist the patio seating, complete with heaters for your alfresco comfort. But the upscale bistro fare and classy cocktails here are excellent inside and out.

LA VERDAD
Mexican $

☎ 617-351-2580; www.laverdadtaque ria.com; 1 Lansdowne St; ☼ lunch, dinner to 2am; ⓡ Kenmore; Ⓥ Ⓖ
This unexpectedly authentic and affordable place on Lansdowne St is taco-rific. By night, it boasts sidewalk seating and pitchers of margaritas; by day there is a simple lunch counter. At any time, it serves warm chewy tortillas, stuffed with your favorite spicy fillings.

OTHER SIDE COSMIC CAFÉ
Café $

☎ 617-536-8437; 407 Newbury St; ☼ lunch, dinner to 1am; ⓡ Hynes; Ⓥ Ⓖ
As soon as you walk into this funky, punky café, you'll know that you have crossed over to the 'other side.' (The other side of Mass Ave, that is.) Cool, young creative-looking people come here for cold beer, big sandwiches, fruit and veggie drinks and strong coffee.

UBURGER *Burgers* $
☎ 617-536-0448; www.uburger.com; 636 Beacon St; ☼ lunch & dinner; ⓡ Kenmore
Not sure what this name implies. These burgers are for u?

Yes. U choose the toppings that u want? Also true. You'll do a U-turn to get to these burgers? Definitely!

⅄ DRINK

⅄ BLEACHER BAR *Sports Bar*
☎ 617-262-2424; www.bleacher barboston.com; 82A Lansdowne St; 🚇 Kenmore

Tucked under the bleachers at Fenway Park, this classy bar offers a view onto center field (go Jacoby baby!). It's not the best place to actually watch the game, but it's an awesome way to experience America's oldest ballpark, even when the Sox are not playing.

⅄ CASK 'N FLAGON *Sports Bar*
☎ 617-536-4840; www.casknflagon .com; 62 Brookline Ave; 🚇 Kenmore

If you are lucky enough to score a pregame sidewalk seat, you'll have a prime spot from which to watch Lansdowne St reach its frenzied best.

⅄ LOWER DEPTHS *Beer Bar*
☎ 617-266-6662; 476 Commonwealth Ave; 🚇 Kenmore

Come to the Lower Depths for its impressive beer selection and presentation. Enjoy the stylish setting (for a beer bar). But don't pass on the $1 Fenway Franks with exotic $1 toppings.

★ PLAY

☆ BOSTON SYMPHONY ORCHESTRA *Classical Music*
☎ 617-266-1200; www.bso.org; 301 Massachusetts Ave; tickets $30-115; 🚇 Symphony; 🅿 ♿

Near-perfect acoustics at Symphony Hall and the challenging programs of maestro James Levine never fail to please the fans of the Boston Symphony Orchestra, which plays here from October to April. In summer, it's the home of Keith Lockhart and the fun-loving **Boston Pops** (www.bostonpops.org).

☆ CHURCH *Live Rock Music*
☎ 617-236-7600; www.churchofboston .com; 69 Kilmarnock St; cover $10-12; ⏱ 5pm-2am; 🚇 Museum or Kenmore

Go to Church and thank the good Lord that Boston is home to so many cool local bands, which play here every night at 9pm. Also: pool tables, plasma TVs and a slick restaurant.

☆ FENWAY PARK *Spectator Sports*
☎ 617-267-1700; www.redsox.com; 4 Yawkey Way; bleacher seats $25-30, grandstand $50; 🚇 Kenmore; ♿ 🧸

Boston's most cherished landmark? Site of the greatest dramas and worst defeats? It's tiny old Fenway Park, home of the Boston Red Sox. Seeing the Red Sox at

Fenway is a highlight of any visit to Boston, but tickets are hard to come by (unless you are willing to pay big bucks to scalpers). Another option is to take the **tour** (adult/child $12/10; ☷ 9am-4pm Apr-Oct, 10am-3pm Nov-Mar), which allows you inside the press box and up on top of the Monster. Avoid afternoon tours on game days.

⭐ HOUSE OF BLUES
Live Rock Music

☎ 888-693-2583; www.hob.com/boston; 15 Lansdowne St; cover $20-30; 🚇 Kenmore; ♿

This new venue on Lansdowne St has already seen the likes of the reunited J Geils Band, BB King, George Clinton, George Thorogood, the Gypsy Kings and the Dropkick Murphys. Standing room only; two levels. Dig the gospel brunch on Sundays.

EMERALD NECKLACE
The Emerald Necklace is an evocative name for a series of parks and green spaces that weaves through Boston, some 7 miles from the Boston Common to Franklin Park. Designed by Frederick Law Olmsted in the late 19th century, the Emerald Necklace treats city residents to a bit of fresh air, green grass and flowing water, right within the city limits. For more information, check out the **Emerald Necklace Conservancy** (www.emeraldnecklace.org).

⭐ HUNTINGTON THEATRE COMPANY *Theater*

☎ 617-266-0800; www.huntingtontheatre.org; 264 Huntington Ave (Boston University Theatre); 🚇 Symphony

This highly acclaimed theater company has staged so many award-winning performances that it's hard to keep track. Many plays by August Wilson, Tom Stoppard and Christopher Durang were premiered here, before going on to fame in the Big Apple.

⭐ JILLIAN'S BILLIARD CLUB & LUCKY STRIKE LANES *Billiards & Bowling*

☎ 617-437-0300; www.jilliansboston.com; 145 Ipswich St; ☷ 11-2am Mon-Sat, noon-2am Sun; 🚇 Kenmore Sq; 🅿

Dress to impress when you go to shoot some pool, knock some pins and ogle members of the opposite sex. Never fear, there does not seem to be any correlation between your bowling score and your ability to score.

⭐ PARADISE LOUNGE
Live Rock Music

☎ 617-562-8800; www.thedise.com; 967-969 Commonwealth Ave; 🚇 Pleasant St

One of Boston's most legendary rock clubs, where you can get up close and personal with some big names. The newish lounge has a hip, cozy atmosphere and a limited menu.

>CAMBRIDGE

Cambridge is sometimes called the 'People's Republic' for its left-leaning politics. A popular T-shirt boasts '02138 – America's most liberal zip code.' There's no doubt about it: on issues from environmental policy to gay marriage and beyond, Cambridge embraces progressive causes.

It was not always that way. The Puritans founded Harvard College in Newtowne (now Cambridge) so the seminarians would stay close, under the watchful eye of the evangelical Reverend Thomas Shepard.

No other event has so defined this city. With the presence of Harvard, Cambridge established early on its reputation as a fertile ground for intellectual and political thought – a reputation it has upheld over 350 years and counting. The addition of the Massachusetts Institute of Technology (MIT) only added to its braininess. Most importantly, thousands of student residents guarantee the city's continued vibrancy and diversity.

CAMBRIDGE

◎ SEE
Harvard Art Museum
  (Future Site) 1 D4
Harvard Art Museum
  (Re-View) 2 D4
Harvard Museum of
  Natural History 3 D2
Harvard Yard 4 C4
Longfellow National
  Historic Site 5 A3
Peabody Museum of
  Archaeology &
  Ethnology ....(see 3)

⬒ SHOP
Cambridge Artists
  Cooperative 6 B4
Curious George Goes
  to Wordsworth 7 B4

Garage 8 C5
Globe Corner
  Bookstore 9 B5
Harvard Bookstore 10 C5
Raven Used Books 11 B5
Tayrona 12 D5
WardMaps.com ....(see 13)

🍴 EAT
Café Pamplona 13 D5
Cambridge, 1 ....14 B4
Casablanca 15 B4
Market in the Square ...16 B4
Mr Bartley's Burger
  Cottage 17 D5
Red House 18 B5
Upstairs on the
  Square 19 B5
Veggie Planet ....(see 25)

▼ DRINK
Algiers Coffee
  House ....(see 15)
Charlie's Kitchen 20 B5
Grendel's Den 21 B5
LA Burdick
  Chocolates 22 B4

★ PLAY
American Repertory
  Theater 23 B4
Brattle Theatre 24 B4
Club Passim 25 B4
Comedy Studio 26 D5
Lizard Lounge 27 C1
Regattabar 28 B5
Zero Arrow Theater 29 D5

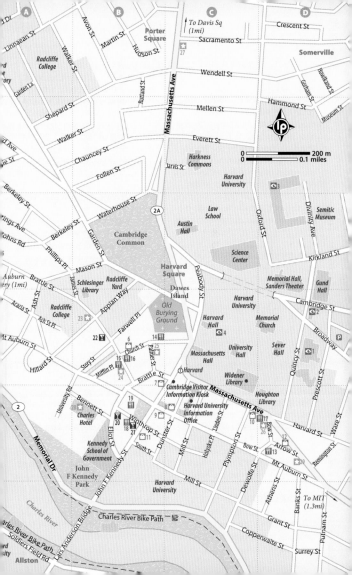

◉ SEE

◉ HARVARD ART MUSEUM

☎ 617-495-9400; www.harvardart museum.org; 485 Broadway; admission free; ◷ 9am-5pm; ⊕ Harvard; ♿

The main building for the Harvard Art Museum (32 Quincy St) is in the midst of a massive renovation, expected to end in 2013. In the meantime, a small but scintillating portion of the collection is on display in an exhibit entitled *Re-View*. Think of it as a sort of Greatest Hits.

◉ HARVARD MUSEUM OF NATURAL HISTORY & PEABODY MUSEUM OF ARCHAEOLOGY & ETHNOLOGY

☎ 617-495-3045; www.hmnh.harvard .edu; 26 Oxford St; adult/concession $9/6- 7; ◷ 9am-5pm; ⊕ Harvard; ♿ ♿

At the intersection of art and science, the famous botanical galleries at HMNH feature more than 3000 pieces of handblown-glass flowers and plants. There are also sparkling gemstones from around the world, an impressive fossil collection and an unbelievable number of stuffed animals. Next door, the Peabody Museum features exhibits about indigenous cultures throughout the Americas.

◉ HARVARD YARD

☎ 617-495-1573; www.harvard.edu; ◷ tours 10am & 2pm Mon-Fri, 2pm Sat, additional tours in summer; ⊕ Harvard

Harvard Yard is the geographic heart of the university, where redbrick buildings and leaf-covered paths exude academia. See the sculpture of John Harvard (aka the statue of three lies), the stately steps of Widener Library and the hallowed Harvard Hall. Take a free campus tour from Holyoke Center.

◉ LONGFELLOW NATIONAL HISTORIC SITE

☎ 617-876-4491; www.nps.gov/long; 105 Brattle St; adult/child $3/free; ◷ house 10am-4:30pm Wed-Sun May-Oct, grounds dawn-dusk year-round; ⊕ Harvard

For 45 years, the elegant yellow mansion on Brattle St was the home of poet Henry Wadsworth Longfellow. Today, the National Historic Site contains many of Longfellow's belongings and lush period gardens.

◉ MOUNT AUBURN CEMETERY

☎ 617-547-7105; www.mountauburn .org; 580 Mt Auburn St; admission free, guided tours $5; ◷ 8am-5pm Oct-Apr, to 7pm May-Sep; ⊕ Harvard; ℗

West of Harvard Sq, this contemplative spot is the country's first 'garden cemetery.' Maps pinpoint the rare botanical specimens and notable burial plots, including those for many political and cultural luminaries. Take bus 71 or 73 from Harvard Sq.

SHOP

CAMBRIDGE ARTISTS COOPERATIVE *Arts & Crafts*

☎ 617-868-4434; www.cambridge
artistscoop.com; 59A Church St;
🕑 10am-6pm Tue, Wed, Fri & Sat, to
8pm Thu, noon-5pm Sun; 🚇 Harvard

Here you'll find three floors of
handmade jewelry, woven scarves,
leather products, pottery and
other arts and crafts made and
sold by local artists.

CURIOUS GEORGE GOES TO WORDSWORTH
Children's Bookstore

☎ 617-498-0062; www.curiousg.com;
1 John F Kennedy St; 🕑 10am-7pm;
🚇 Harvard

You can find your favorite story
about that mischievous monkey,
but there are also thousands of
other children's books and toys.

GARAGE *Shopping Mall*

36 John F Kennedy St; 🕑 10am-9pm;
🚇 Harvard

This gritty mini-mall has a food
court, Newbury Comics (p95),
crazy costume store Hootenanny,
and an edgy urban boutique and
skate shop, Proletariat.

GLOBE CORNER BOOKSTORE *Bookstore*

☎ 617-497-6277; www.globecorner
.com; 90 Mt Auburn St; 🕑 9:30am-9pm
Mon-Sat, 11am-6pm Sun; 🚇 Harvard

Travel the globe with books
from the Globe, including travel
literature, guidebooks and maps,
as well as books by your favorite
Lonely Planet author.

HARVARD BOOKSTORE
Bookstore

☎ 617-661-1515; www.harvard.com;
1256 Massachusetts Ave; 🕑 9am-11pm
Mon-Sat, 10am-10pm Sun; 🚇 Harvard

Harvard Bookstore is not officially
affiliated with the university, but
it is the university community's
favorite place to browse. The shop
also hosts book talks and other
events. Used and bargain books
are in the basement.

The Harvard Bookstore is a local favorite

📖 RAVEN USED BOOKS
Secondhand Bookstore

☎ 617-441-6999; www.ravencambridge
.com; 52B John F Kennedy St;
🕑 10am-9pm Mon-Sat, 11am-8pm Sun;
🚇 Harvard

Tucked into a tiny basement, Raven knows its audience: its 14,000 titles focus on scholarly titles, especially in the liberal arts. Bibliophiles agree that the quality and condition of books is top-notch.

📷 TAYRONA
Jewelry & Accessories

☎ 617-661-4267; www.tayrona1156
.com; 1156 Massachusetts Ave; 🕑 10am-
7pm Mon-Sat; 🚇 Harvard

One of many H-Square boutiques with international panache. Exquisite jewelry, beaded handbags, batik scarves and handcrafted gift items reflect an exotic but thoroughly sophisticated style.

📷 WARDMAPS.COM *Maps*

☎ 617-497-0737; www.wardmaps.com;
12 Bow St; 🕑 9am-6pm Mon, Tue & Fri,
to 7pm Wed & Thu, 12-6pm Sat, to 5pm
Sun; 🚇 Harvard

Maps are maps. But at WardMaps, they are also coffee mugs, mouse pads, notebooks and greeting cards, crafted from the reproduction antique or contemporary map of your choice.

🍴 EAT

🍴 CAFÉ PAMPLONA *Café* $

☎ 617-492-0352; 12 Bow St; 🕑 lunch
& dinner Mon-Sat, 2pm-1am Sun;
🚇 Harvard

Located in a cozy cellar on a backstreet, this no-frills European café is the choice among old-time Cantabrigians for coffee, tea or a light meal. The tiny terrace is a delight in summer.

WORTH THE TRIP: MIT

The MIT campus offers a novel perspective on Cambridge academia: proudly nerdy, but not quite as tweedy as Harvard. MIT seems to pride itself on being offbeat. Wander into a courtyard and you might find it is graced with a sculpture by Henry Moore or Alexander Calder; or you might just as well find a Ping-Pong table or a trampoline. It's worth a wander to see what they'll come up with next. Alternatively, join an excellent **guided campus tour** (10:45am & 2:45pm Mon-Fri), which departs from the information center. Sites of note on campus:
List Visual Arts Center (☎ 617-253-4680; http://web.mit.edu/lvac; Weisner Bldg, 20 Ames St; suggested donation $5; 🕑 noon-6pm Tue, Wed & Fri-Sun, to 8pm Thu; 🚇 Kendall/MIT; 🅿 🚻 🔥) Exploring the boundaries of artistic inquiry.
MIT Museum (☎ 617-253-4444; http://web.mit.edu/museum; 265 Massachusetts Ave; adult/child $7.50/3; 🕑 10am-5pm; 🚇 Central; 🅿 🚻 🔥) Featuring an intriguing robot exhibit.

🍴 CAMBRIDGE, 1 *Pizzeria* $$
☎ 617-576-1111; www.cambridge1
.us; 27 Church St; ⏱ lunch & dinner;
🚇 Harvard

The old fire station has been
turned into a sleek, stylish pizzeria.
The menu is pretty simple: nine
pizzas, five salads and one dessert,
each of which is uniquely delicious.

🍴 CASABLANCA
Mediterranean $$
☎ 617-876-0999; www.casablancarestau
rant.com; 40 Brattle St; ⏱ lunch, dinner to
1am or 2am Mon-Sat; 🚇 Harvard

Below the Brattle Theatre, this Har-
vard Sq classic has long been the
hangout of film fans, local literati
and other arty types. Regulars skip
the formal dining room and slip in
the back door to the boisterous bar.

🍴 MARKET IN THE SQUARE
Cafeteria $
☎ 617-441-2000; 60 Church St; ⏱ 24hr;
🚇 Harvard; 🖥 Ⓥ ♿

Anyone who has ever pulled an
all-nighter will appreciate this
24-hour establishment. The self-
service cafeteria is well stocked
with fresh salads, soups and hot
dishes.

🍴 MR BARTLEY'S BURGER
COTTAGE *Burgers* $
☎ 617-354-6559; www.mrbartley.com;
1246 Massachusetts Ave; ⏱ lunch &
dinner; 🚇 Harvard; ♿

A Harvard Sq institution, Bartley's
has at least 40 different burgers.
If none of those suits your fancy,
create your own masterpiece. PS
Don't forget the sweet-potato fries.

🍴 RED HOUSE *International* $$
☎ 617-576-0605; www.redhouse.com;
98 Winthrop St; ⏱ lunch & dinner Tue-
Sun, to 1am Fri & Sat; 🚇 Harvard

Reminiscent of an old-fashioned
inn, the former Cox-Hicks house
retains its historic charm with
its wide-plank wood floors and
functioning fireplace. In summer,
the draw is the patio overlooking a
quiet corner of Harvard Sq.

🍴 UPSTAIRS ON THE SQUARE
International $$$
☎ 617-864-1933; www.upstairsonthe
square.com; 91 Winthrop St; ⏱ lunch,
dinner to 1am; 🚇 Harvard

Upstairs on the Square is all about
glamour and glitz, creativity and
selectivity. The downstairs Monday
Club Bar offers lunch in a more
casual atmosphere, with a slightly
cheaper menu and a wall of win-
dows overlooking Winthrop Park.

🍸 DRINK
🍸 ALGIERS COFFEE HOUSE
Café
☎ 617-492-1557; 40 Brattle St; ⏱ 8am-
midnight; 🚇 Harvard

Upstairs from the Brattle Theatre,
this secret hideaway is an irresistible

spot to settle in with a book and your drink of choice (beer, wine, coffee, frappe).

Y CHARLIE'S KITCHEN
Dive Bar
☎ 617-492-9646; 10 Eliot St;
🚇 Harvard
Drink Pabst Blue Ribbon and eat patty burgers and lobster rolls, while bumping the tattooed elbows of your screaming neighbors. They are screaming because the rock-and-roll music is blaring from the jukebox at inordinate volumes.

Y GRENDEL'S DEN *Pub*
☎ 617-491-1160; www.grendelsden
.com; 89 Winthrop St; 🚇 Harvard

This space really does feel like a den – dark and cozy with a fire going on cold days. The service is friendly, the beer is cold and – best of all – the tasty pub grub is half-price from 5pm to 7pm.

Y LA BURDICK CHOCOLATES
Café
☎ 617-491-4340; www.burdickchoco
late.com; 52D Brattle St; 🕒 8am-9pm
Mon-Thu, to 10pm Fri & Sat, 9am-9pm
Sun; 🚇 Harvard
This is really a boutique chocolate store. But there are a few tiny tables, where patrons sit and sip delectably rich hot cocoa. Milk or dark chocolate? That may be the most difficult decision of your day.

WORTH THE TRIP: DAVIS SQUARE
Since Somerville is populated by lots of 20-somethings and bohemians, it's no surprise that places to drink the hooch have arisen to serve them. Davis Sq is Somerville's bustling and pretty center, providing urban nightlife with a village feel.

Burren (☎ 617-776-6896; 247 Elm St; 🕒 noon-1am; 🚇 Davis) A cavernous Irish pub with live music and free-flowing beer.

Diesel Cafe (☎ 671-629-8717; 257 Elm St; 🕒 7am-midnight Mon-Fri, 8am-midnight Sat & Sun; 🚇 Davis) One of Boston's best coffeehouses, Diesel attracts a regular patronage of lesbians.

Redbones (☎ 617-628-2200; www.redbones.com; 55 Chester St; 🕒 11:30am-12:30am; 🚇 Davis) Huge portions of barbecue ribs and huge selections of beers.

Sacco's Bowl Haven (☎ 617-776-0552; www.saccosbowlhaven.com; 45 Day St; game/ shoe rental $3/1.50; 🕒 10am-midnight Mon-Sat, noon-11:30pm Sun; 🚇 Davis; 👶) A time warp of a bowling alley that was last renovated c 1950. Candlepin bowling, no alcohol.

Somerville Theatre (☎ 617-625-5700; www.somervilletheatreonline.com; 55 Davis Sq; adult/senior/matinee $8/5/7; 🚇 Davis) A classic art-deco theater with plenty of gilding and pastel murals of muses, plus a balcony in the main hall. Shows Hollywood hits and live music.

Adam Roffman
Program Director of the Independent Film Festival of Boston, set decorator for many Boston-based productions, moviemaker and movie lover

Why is Boston an attractive destination for filmmakers? The tax incentives offered by the Commonwealth and the quality of the crew. Plus, Boston is a historic city with architecture that would otherwise have to be built from scratch. **Best Boston movie** *Gone Baby Gone*. **Why IFFBoston has taken off** Boston has a well-educated, artistic population that appreciates the fact that independent film does not get dumbed down. It tells complicated stories in new and different ways. **Best place to meet people in film** Attend the IFFBoston (p27). Festival participants hang out at Clink and Alibi (p53). Everybody plays at least one round at Sacco's Bowl Haven (opposite). **Best place for dinner and a movie** Redbone's (opposite) and the Somerville Theatre (opposite).

PLAY

⭐ AMERICAN REPERTORY THEATER *Theater*

☎ 617-547-8300; www.amrep.org; 64 Brattle St; tickets $40-75; 🚇 Harvard

The prestigious ART stages new plays and experimental interpretations of classics. It also has performance space at the **Zero Arrow Theater** (cnr Massachusetts Ave & Arrow St; 🚇 Harvard), which is used for both cabaret-style and more traditional performances.

⭐ BRATTLE THEATRE *Cinema*

☎ 617-876-6837; www.brattlefilm .org; 40 Brattle St; adult/child/student $9.50/6.50/8, matinee $8; 🚇 Harvard

The Brattle is a film lover's 'cinema *paradiso*.' Film noir, independent films and thematic series are shown in this renovated 1890 repertory theater.

⭐ CLUB PASSIM *Folk Music*

☎ 617-492-7679; www.clubpassim.org; 47 Palmer St; tickets $10-15; 🚇 Harvard

Club Passim is sustaining Boston's folk scene, with top-notch local and national acts. Also onsite is the restaurant **Veggie Planet** (☎ 617-661-1513; www.veggieplanet .net; 47 Palmer St; 🚇 Harvard; **V**), which is undeniably excellent for herbivores.

⭐ COMEDY STUDIO *Comedy*

☎ 617-661-6507; www.thecomedy studio.com; 1238 Massachusetts Ave; admission $8-10; ⏱ 8pm Tue-Sun; 🚇 Harvard

Upstairs from the Hong Kong restaurant, this low-budget comedy house has a reputation for hosting cutting-edge acts. This is where talented future stars refine their racy material.

⭐ LIZARD LOUNGE *Live Music*

☎ 617-547-0759; www.lizardloungeclub .com; 1667 Massachusetts Ave; cover $5-10; ⏱ 9pm-1am Mon, 7:30pm-1am Tue & Wed, to 2am Thu-Sat, to 1am Sun; 🚇 Harvard

This small space doubles as both a jazz and rock venue, with some off-beat evenings like the Sunday poetry slam and Monday open-mic challenge. The interior is done up with red lights and upholstery along with good-looking people.

⭐ REGATTABAR *Jazz Club*

☎ 617-395-7757; www.regattabarjazz .com; 1 Bennett St; tickets $15-35; 🚇 Harvard; **P**

Regattabar looks a lot like a conference room in a hotel – in this case the Charles Hotel. The décor may be drab but it's an intimate space to see some pretty big names in jazz.

The *Mayflower II* is a life-size replica of the Pilgrims' vessel (p127)

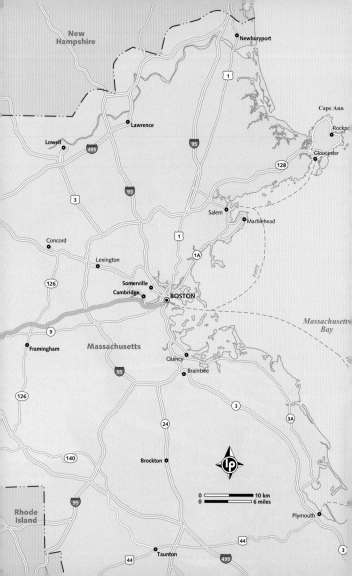

LEXINGTON & CONCORD

Church steeples and ancient oaks give these western towns a stateliness that belies the drama that occurred centuries ago. White churches and historic taverns surround the historic **Battle Green** in Lexington. Here, the skirmish between patriots and British troops jumpstarted the War for Independence. **Buckman Tavern** (☎ 781-862-5598; 1 Bedford Rd; adult/child $5/3; ☻ 10am-5pm Mon-Sat, 1-5pm Sun Apr-Oct) was the Minuteman headquarters.

Two miles west, the British route to Concord has been designated the **Minuteman National Historic Park**. The **visitors center** (☎ 978-862-7753; www.nps .gov/mima; ☻ 9am-5pm Apr-Oct) at the park's eastern end shows a multimedia presentation depicting Paul Revere's ride and the ensuing battles. Within the park, **Battle Rd** is a wooded trail that connects the historic sites – from Meriam's Corner to the Paul Revere capture site. A half-mile north of Concord center, the **Old North Bridge** is the site of the 'shot heard around the world' (as Ralph Waldo Emerson wrote in his poem 'Concord Hymn').

There are a string of museums along Lexington Rd, southeast of Concord center, including the homes of local authors Ralph Waldo Emerson and Louisa May Alcott. The **Concord Museum** (☎ 978-369-9609; www.concord museum.org; 200 Lexington Rd; adult/child/senior & student $10/5/8; ☻ 9am-5pm Mon-Sat & noon-5pm Sun Apr-Dec, 11am-4pm Mon-Sat & 1-4pm Sun Jan-Mar) contains an enormous collection of Henry David Thoreau artifacts. All of these literary figures rest in **Sleepy Hollow Cemetery** (☎ 978-371-6299; Bedford St).

End the day by following in Thoreau's footsteps to **Walden Pond** (☎ 978-369-3254; www.mass.gov/dem/parks/wldn.htm; 915 Walden St; admission free; ☻ dawn-dusk; ℗), a serene spot surrounded by acres of forest. Parking costs $5.

INFORMATION

Location 12 miles to 20 miles west of Boston
Getting There To Lexington, take bus No 62 or 76 from Alewife T station or ride 6 miles along the Minuteman Bikeway. To Concord, commuter rail trains ($6.50, 40 minutes, eight daily) run from North Station.
Contact Lexington Visitor Center (☎ 781-862-2480; www.lexingtonchamber.org; 1875 Mass Ave; ☻ 9am-5pm Apr-Nov, 10am-4pm Dec-Mar); Concord Visitors Center (☎ 978-369-3120; www.concordchamberofcommerce.org; 58 Main St; ☻ 9:30am-4:30pm Apr-Oct)
Eating Try Main Streets Market (☎ 888-493-3981; 42 Main St, Concord; ☻ 6:30am-6pm daily, dinner Tue-Sat; Ⓥ) or Via Lago (☎ 781-861-6174; 1845 Massachusetts Ave, Lexington; ☻ 7am-9pm Mon-Sat; Ⓥ).

DAY TRIPS

SALEM

This town's very name conjures images of witchcraft and women being burned at the stake during the famous witch trials of 1692. Indeed, Salem goes all out at Halloween (see p29). The most authentic of more than a score of witchy sites is **Witch House** (☎ 978-744-8815; www.salemweb.com/witchhouse; 310 Essex St; adult/child/senior $8/4/6; ☿ 10am-5pm May-Nov, longer hrs in Oct). This was the home of Jonathan Corwin, a local magistrate who investigated witchcraft claims. There are a covey of other witch museums are around town.

The **House of the Seven Gables** (☎ 978-744-0991; www.7gables.org; 54 Turner St; adult/child/senior $12/7.25/11; ☿ 10am-5pm Nov-Jun, to 7pm Jul-Oct) was made famous in Nathaniel Hawthorne's 1851 novel, which brings to life the gloomy Puritan atmosphere of early New England.

The witch phenomena obscure Salem's true claim to fame: its glory days as a center for the clipper-ship trade with China. The **Salem Maritime National Historic Site** (☎ 978-740-1660; www.nps.gov/sama; 193 Derby St; admission free; ☿ 9am-5pm) comprises the custom house, the wharves and the other buildings along Derby St that are remnants of this thriving shipping industry.

Many Salem vessels followed the route around the Cape of Good Hope, and soon the East India Marine Society was founded. The company's charter required the establishment of a museum 'to house the natural and artificial curiosities' brought back by member ships. The collection was the basis for the world-class **Peabody Essex Museum** (☎ 866-745-1876, 978-745-1876; www.pem.org; Essex St Mall, New Liberty St; adult/child/student/senior $15/free/11/13; ☿ 10am-5pm). Predictably, it is strong on Asian art and includes **Yin Yu Tang** (adult/child $5/free), a house that was shipped from southeastern China.

INFORMATION

Location 20 miles northeast of Boston

Getting There Both the Newburyport and Rockport lines of the commuter rail run from North Station ($5.25, 30 minutes). Salem Ferry (www.salemferry.com) operates a commuter service to Central Wharf (round-trip adult/child/senior $22/14/18).

Contact Destination Salem (☎ 978-744-0004; www.salem.org; 63 Wharf St) or the NPS Regional Visitor Center (☎ 978-740-1650; 2 Liberty St; ☿ 9am-5pm)

Eating Front Street Coffeehouse (☎ 978-740-6697; 20 Front St; ☿ 7am-7pm; 💻) is a cool place to sip a caffe latte or munch on a sandwich. Or try Rockmore Floating Restaurant (☎ 978-740-1001; www.rockmore.com; Pickering Wharf; ☿ 11am-9pm Jun-Aug). That's right: floating. Catch the free shuttle to here from the Congress St Bridge, but don't forget to tip the captain.

PLYMOUTH

Thousands of visitors come here each year to look at the weathered Plymouth Rock and to consider what it was like for the Pilgrims, who stepped ashore this strange land in the autumn of 1620. To learn more, climb aboard **Mayflower II** (☎ 508-746-1622; State Pier; adult/child/senior $8/6/7; ✆ 9am-5pm Apr-Nov), a replica of the small ship in which they made the fateful voyage. A combo ticket for *Mayflower II* and Plimoth Plantation (below) is available (adult/child/senior $25/15/22).

In the winter of 1620–21, half of the Pilgrims died of disease, privation and exposure to the elements. But new arrivals joined the survivors and by 1627 Plymouth colony was on the road to prosperity. The **Plimoth Plantation** (☎ 508-746-1622; MA 3A; adult/child/senior $21/12/19; ✆ 9am-5:30pm Apr-Nov), a mile south of Plymouth Rock, authentically re-creates the Pilgrims' 1627 settlement, with everything in the village painstakingly researched and remade. **Hobbamock's (Wampanoag) Homesite** replicates the life of a Native American community in the area at the same time. Less authentic, but more celebratory, is America's Hometown Thanksgiving Celebration (p30).

Claiming to be the oldest continually operating public museum in the country, **Pilgrim Hall Museum** (☎ 508-746-1620; www.pilgrimhall.org; 75 Court St; adult/child/senior $6/3/5; ✆ 9:30am-4:30pm Feb-Dec) was founded in 1824. At the opposite end of town, the **Jenney Grist Mill** (☎ 508-747-4544; www.jenneygristmill.org; 6 Spring Lane; adult/child $6/4; ✆ 9:30am-5pm Mon-Sat, noon-5pm Sun Apr-Nov) is located on the site of the first grist mill, established in 1636. As New England's oldest European community, Plymouth also has its share of fine old houses, one of which is the **Mayflower Society Museum** (☎ 508-746-2590; www.themayflowersociety.com; 4 Winslow St; ✆ 10am-4pm daily Jul & Aug, Sat & Sun Jun & Sep-Oct).

INFORMATION
Location 40 miles south of Boston
Getting There MBTA commuter trains ($7.75, one hour, four daily) to Plymouth leave from South Station. GATRA buses connect the P&B terminal and the train station at Cordage Park to the town center.
Contact Destination Plymouth (☎ 508-747-7533; www.visit-plymouth.com; 170 Water St; ✆ 9am-5pm Apr-Nov, to 8pm Jun-Aug) Located at the rotary across from Plymouth Harbor.
Eating Jubilee (☎ 508-747-3700; 22 Court St; ✆ lunch & dinner) serves soups, salads and pastas, while the Lobster Hut (☎ 508-746-2270; Town Wharf; ✆ lunch & dinner) dishes up big plates of fried clams, fish and chips, and lobster in all shapes and sizes.

Peak inside Boston's many subcultures to see what's in there for you. Eating, drinking and sleeping are obligatory, but that's only the beginning. Paint a picture, sing a song, tell a joke, explore an island, ride a bike, reenact the revolution, run a marathon…and by all means, root for the Red Sox.

The stunning interior of the Isabella Stewart Gardner Museum (p110)

ACCOMMODATIONS

Boston offers a complete range of accommodations, from dorms and hostels, to inviting guesthouses in historic quarters, to swanky hotels with all the amenities.

When considering your options, think about transportation. Easy access to the T puts the entire city at your disposal in 30 minutes. That said, Boston is a highly walkable city, and all of these central neighborhoods offer their own array of sights and shops, restaurants and bars.

Site of the Massachusetts State House and steps from the Public Garden, Beacon Hill combines history and greenery. A short stroll across the Common lands you on the Freedom Trail and the city's major tourist attractions; but Beacon Hill is also a lived-in (if luxuriously so) residential neighborhood, with some of the city's best restaurants and antique shops.

Downtown, Tremont St is an attractive address for tourists. The Freedom Trail goes right past your front door, and the city's major sights and best restaurants are a few steps away. With the completion of the Big Dig, the Waterfront has been reconnected to the rest of the city, making it a foot-friendly place to stay, especially for early birds who might like to watch the sun rise over the harbor.

Across the Fort Point Channel, the Seaport District is a bit removed from the action. But it's nirvana for seafood eaters and art connoisseurs. Bonus: it's also an easy trip from the airport.

Ranging from affordable to extravagant, the hotels in the Theater District are excellent options for culture vultures. And isn't it nice to have Chinatown nearby when you get the munchies at 2am?

 Hotels & Hostels

Need a place to stay? Find and book it at lonelyplanet.com. Over 110 properties are featured for Boston – each personally visited, thoroughly reviewed and happily recommended by a Lonely Planet author. From hostels to high-end hotels, we've hunted out the places that will bring you unique and special experiences. Read independent reviews by authors and other travelers, and get practical information including amenities, maps and photos. Then reserve your room simply and securely via Hotels & Hostels – our online booking service. It's all at lonelyplanet.com/hotels.

In the Back Bay, expense-account travelers can take their pick from the many fancy places clustered around Copley Sq. The residential streets are also home to some friendly guesthouses, which allow travelers to experience all the charm and convenience of this neighborhood without spending a fortune. Particularly good deals are hidden on the edge of the South End, Boston's gay-friendliest neighborhood. It's not the most accessible place to stay, but it is home to avant-garde art galleries and daring new restaurants – thus it's a destination in its own right.

Considering that Boston is a city filled with students, there are surprisingly few accommodation options targeting budget travelers. But Fenway and Kenmore Sq are exceptions. Home to myriad students and the sacred haunt of Red Sox fans, this area has a bunch of inexpensive places to stay. (For late-night clubbers, this may be your best bet for stumbling home without the aid of a taxi.)

Cambridge has its own collection of quaint B&Bs and upscale hotels. The red line guarantees a short and convenient commute into the city for serious sightseeing, but Harvard Sq and Central Sq also boast vibrant cultural scenes of their own.

BEST ROOMS WITH A VIEW
> Liberty Hotel (www.libertyhotel.com)
> Gryphon House (www.innboston.com)
> Nine Zero (www.ninezero.com)
> Boston Harbor Hotel (www.bhh.com)
> Marriott's Custom House (www.marriott.com)

BEST ROOMS WITH VALUE
> Harding House (www.cambridgeinns.com)
> Newbury Guesthouse (www.newburyguesthouse.com)
> Oasis Guest House (www.oasisgh.com)
> College Club (www.collegeclubofboston.com)
> John Jeffries House (www.johnjeffrieshouse.com)

BEST GAY STAYS
> Clarendon Square Inn (www.clarendonsquare.com)
> Taylor House (www.taylorhouse.com)
> Back Bay Hotel (formerly Jurys Boston; www.doylecollection.com)
> Encore (www.encorebandb.com)
> Chandler Inn (www.chandlerinn.com)

BEST GREEN SCENES
> Irving House (www.irvinghouse.com)
> Seaport Hotel (www.seaportboston.com)
> Hostelling International Boston (www.bostonhostel.org)
> Royal Sonesta (www.sonesta.com)
> Lenox Hotel (www.lenoxhotel.com)

DRINK

Despite the grave of Cotton Mather, modern-day Bostonians like to get their drink on. Blame (or thank) the Irish immigrants for cultivating Boston's taste for beer. Now Boston is home to the largest beer brewer in the United States (Sam Adams), as well as Harpoon and a host of microbreweries.

Perhaps that means it was the Italian influence that has encouraged the oenophiles, who now sip pinot grigio and Nero D'Avola at wine bars all around the city. And what about the burgeoning cocktail scene, which is among the hottest in the country?

Lacking an adequate explanation, we prefer to pour ourselves a drink and raise a toast to our friendly neighborhood barkeep for keeping our whistles whetted.

Boston's drinking scene is dominated by four categories of venues: dive bars, Irish bars (some more authentic than others), sports bars and a new breed of truly hip cocktail bars. Many of the sweeter spots are outside the center, including in Cambridge and Somerville. If you're stuck on the Boston peninsula, get away from the Freedom Trail – a desolate wasteland if you're looking to imbibe in style – and head to the South End (gay-friendly), Back Bay (yuppies and students) or Chinatown (the diviest of dives). A notable exception to the Freedom Trail rule is the North End, where a handful of cafés serve coffee and Campari along Hanover St.

Get the inside scoop on drinking in Boston by reading Lauren Clark's excellent informative blog, www.drinkboston.com, a guide to bars, bartenders and imbibing in Boston.

SNAPSHOTS

BEST FOR BEER

> Boston Beer Works (p53)
> Bukowski Tavern (p98)
> Lower Depths (p112)

BEST FOR WINE

> Troquet (p88)
> Navy Yard Bistro & Wine Bar (p43)
> Bin 26 Enoteca (p62)
> Bina Osteria (p72)
> Piattini (p97)

BEST FOR COCKTAILS

> Flash's Cocktails (p106)
> Drink (p81)
> Eastern Standard (p110)
> Marliave (p73)
> 28 Degrees (p106)

BEST FOR SPORTS

> Bleacher Bar (p112)
> Caffé dello Sport (p54)
> Cask 'n Flagon (p112)
> Fritz (p106)
> Johnnie's on the Side (p54)

Top left Microbrewery Boston Beer Works (p53) **Above** Red Sox fans warm up at the Cask 'n Flagon before a game (p112)

FOOD

With a nickname like Beantown, you know that Boston is into food.

First of all, let's get that little bit of history out of the way. Culinary historians believe that Native Americans cooked beans with fatty bear meat and molasses in earthenware pots. Early settlers likely adapted this recipe by substituting pork for bear meat, resulting in the famed Boston baked beans. There you have it: Beantown.

Despite the name, you'll have some trouble finding baked beans on a menu in Boston today. The exception is Durgin Park (p72), which specializes in the fare of yesteryear. Also off the menu: boiled dinner (boiled beef with cabbage, carrots and potatoes) and lobster Newburg (creamy lobster served over buttered toast).

Never fear: Boston chefs continue to take advantage of the local bounty. And seafood certainly never goes out of style, especially the 'sacred cod' and various shellfish. But Boston has developed a multifaceted local cuisine, drawing on these unique regional traditions and the richness and variety of its international influences.

The international influence on Boston cuisine cannot be underestimated. Italian, Irish and Portuguese are already old hat. Now Bostonians are sampling Brazilian, Chinese, Indian, Thai and Vietnamese. Immigrants open restaurants to cater to their own community, but these exotic eats are also attracting the attention of well-traveled Bostonians who are curious about global cultures.

In this era of creative culinary discovery, more and more Bostonians are reclaiming their roots in one crucial way: their appreciation of fresh, seasonal and organic products. Frozen foods and canned goods – once liberating – are now anathema, as food-lovers are reminded how much better ingredients taste when they are fresh (and even more so when they are pulled straight from the ground, without chemical fertilization or genetic modification).

There are many online resources for foodies who want to know more about shopping, cooking and eating in Boston. **Edible Boston** (www.edible boston.net) is a magazine about local food and the people who produce it, cook it and eat it. Local foodie blogs include **Urban Spoon** (www.urbanspoon .com) and the **Boston Foodie** (http://thebostonfoodie.blogspot.com). And of course there's always **Chowhound** (http://chowhound.chow.com).

BEST EAT STREETS
> Hanover St (p50)
> Tremont St (p103)
> Charles St (p62)
> Tyler St (p84)

BEST FOR VEGETARIAN
> Grezzo (p51)
> My Thai Vegan Café (p86)
> Other Side Cosmic Café (p111)
> Veggie Planet (p122)

BEST FOR LATE-NIGHT
> Parish Café & Bar (p97)
> Casablanca (p119)
> Franklin Café (p104)
> Market in the Square (p119)
> Suishaya (p87)

BEST FOR BRUNCH
> Emperor's Garden (p87)
> Gaslight, Brasserie du Coin (p104)
> Toro (p105)
> Union Bar & Grille (p105)

Above Faneuil Hall (p68) and Quincy Market (p73) offer a wide array of Boston's quintessential cuisines

HISTORY

The Cradle of Liberty. The Hub of the Universe. The Athens of America. These are big words for a midsized city. But Boston lives up to them. With its rich history, grand architecture and world-renowned academic and cultural institutions, the city retains and radiates the glory it has garnered over the last four centuries.

It was the Puritans who set out in search of religious freedom and founded Boston as their 'shining city on a hill.' In the following century, the Sons of Liberty caroused and rabble-roused until the colonies found themselves in the midst of a War for Independence. A hundred years later, it was Boston's poets and philosophers who were leading a cultural revolution – pushing progressive causes such as abolitionism, feminism and transcendentalism.

For all intents and purposes, Boston is the oldest city in America. And you can hardly walk a step over her cobblestone streets without running into historic sites, many of which are overseen by the **Bostonian Society** (www.bostonhistory.org).

There is no one museum that tells the stories and displays the relics from Boston's history – although there are plans to build a new **Boston Museum** (www.bostonmuseum.org) by 2012.

In the meantime, the Freedom Trail (p14) winds its way around the city, connecting 16 sites of varying historical significance. Many are museums; some are monuments; and others are churches, cemeteries and old buildings of note. They do contain artifacts and exhibits but more importantly, these are the very places where history unfolded. In effect, Boston is one enormous outdoor history museum, where visitors can remember and relive the events of centuries past.

Each neighborhood tells its own dramatic tales. Beacon Hill was the center of the abolitionist movement and a crucial stop on the Underground Railroad, a history that is depicted at the Museum of Afro-American History (p59) and along the Black Heritage Trail (p58). Cambridge boasts an equally long and legendary past, most palpable on the grounds of the country's oldest university (p116) or in the mansions along Tory Row (p116).

Indeed, everywhere you turn, you will spot commemorative plaques and historical markers, reminders of bygone eras. Bygone but not forgotten.

BEST STOPS ON THE FREEDOM TRAIL
> Boston Common (p58)
> Granary Burying Ground (p58)
> Old State House & Massacre Site (p70)
> Old North Church (p48)
> Bunker Hill Monument (p42)

BEST HISTORIC PUBS & RESTAURANTS
> Warren Tavern (p45)
> Union Oyster House (p73)
> Last Hurrah (p74)
> Marliave (p73)
> Red House (p119)

BEST JFK HISTORY
> John F Kennedy Memorial Site (p110)
> John F Kennedy Library & Museum (p78)
> Harvard Yard (p116)
> Union Oyster House (p73)

BEST GRAVE SITES
> John Winthrop, King's Chapel & Burying Ground (p68)
> Cotton Mather, Copp's Hill Burying Ground (p48)
> Paul Revere, Granary Burying Ground (p58)
> Ralph Waldo Emerson, Sleepy Hollow Cemetery (p125)
> Henry Wadsworth Longfellow, Mt Auburn Cemetery (p116)

Above Harvard Yard, at the heart of the US's oldest university, exemplifies Cambridge's long and legendary past (p116)

OUTSIDE

Considering Boston's large student population and extensive green spaces, it's no surprise to see urban outdoorsmen and women running along the Esplanade, cycling the Emerald Necklace and skating the Minuteman Bikeway. For seafaring types, the Charles River and the Boston Harbor offer opportunities for kayaking and canoeing, sailing and sculling, and even swimming in their brisk waters.

Boston is a compact city, which makes it easy to get around on foot. Walking or running the city streets is in fact one of the best ways to get to know the city. Clearly, pounding the pavement is a popular pastime in Boston, where the biggest annual event is a marathon (p27)!

If you prefer to stay off the streets, miles of trails through Boston's parks offer an easy escape from the traffic. The Boston Harbor Islands (p68) also contain unpaved trails to explore.

Cyclists may have a harder time on the streets, especially if they are not used to urban riding, but there are plenty of off-road routes. One of the most popular circuits runs along both sides of the Charles River between the Museum of Science (p48) and the Mt Auburn St Bridge in Watertown (5 miles west of Cambridge). The round-trip is 17 miles, but the 10 bridges in between offer ample opportunity to turn around and shorten the trip. The best of Boston's bicycle trails is the **Minuteman Bikeway** (www.minuteman bikeway.org), which starts in Arlington (near Alewife station), leading 5 miles to historic Lexington center (see p125), then traversing an additional 4 miles of idyllic scenery before it terminates in the rural suburb of Bedford.

You can take your bike on any of the MBTA subway lines except the green and silver lines, but you must avoid rush hours (7am to 10am and 4pm to 7pm weekdays) and always ride on the last train car. For more information contact **Mass Bike** (☎ 617-542-2453; www.massbike.org).

Between the Boston Harbor and the Charles River, boaters have plenty of opportunities to get out on the water. In the last decade, the Charles River has undergone a massive cleanup effort, which has been lauded as successful. Indeed, now the **Charles River Swimming Club** (www.charlesriver swimmingclub.org) hosts the annual Charles River One-Mile Swim, the first open-water swim in Boston's beloved 'dirty water' (see p157). But that does not mean that just anybody can swim in the Charles. The swimming club conducts countless tests, monitors the weather and water flows and makes special arrangements for a safe swimming dock along the Esplanade. The club estimates that the river will not actually be open for public swimming for another 10 years.

The cleanup efforts in the Boston Harbor have yielded more visible results. Beaches in South Boston (p81) and at the Harbor Islands (p68) are sandy, scenic and swimmable – if you can bear the frigid water!

In Boston there is plenty of winter to go around. The snow usually arrives in December and sticks around until March, if not April. While Bostonians maintain a long tradition of whingeing about the weather, they also know how to endure winter: that's right, put on your big boots and your warm, woolly hat and go out and play in the snow. Skating on the Frog Pond (p58) and skiing on the Esplanade (p99) are long-time Boston traditions.

BEST BOATING
> Codzilla (p75)
> Community Boating (p65)
> Courageous Sailing (p45)

BEST CYCLING
> Charles River Route (p99)
> Southwest Corridor Park (p102)
> Minuteman Bikeway (p125)
> Emerald Necklace (p113)

BEST BEACHES
> Spectacle Island (p68)
> Lovells Island (p68)
> Carson Beach (p81)

BEST RACES
> Best Buddies Challenge (www .bestbuddiesmassachusetts.org)
> Boston Marathon (p22; www .bostonmarathon.org)
> Charles River Swimming Club (www .charlesriverswimmingclub.org)
> Head of the Charles (www.hocr.org)
> Tufts 10K for Women (www.tufts healthplan.com/tufts10k)

Top left The Charles River (p99) provides myriad outdoor activity options, including boating (p65)

ART

Boston has long been an artistic hub, with the world-class Museum of Fine Arts (MFA; p110) and the charming Isabella Stewart Gardner Museum (p110) displaying the finest of old-school art in their handsome quarters on the banks of the Muddy River.

But art is a slippery substance. In order to stay relevant, an art scene must be dynamic and daring – it cannot remain confined to its protected place on the walls of a 19th-century palazzo.

In recent years, Boston's contemporary scene has busted its boundaries. The dramatic and enigmatic new home for the ICA (p78) is the most visible sign of this shift. But there is also a trickle-down effect, as awareness grows of the city's artistic prowess. Public interest increases, and artists respond to the demand, offering exhibits and open studios to share their work. The streets south of Washington St used to be a dead zone, but 'SoWa' is now an enticing destination, especially during the monthly First Friday events (p30). An entire neighborhood is growing up around the original art community at Fort Point (p78). Even the MFA is building a new wing in order to expand its contemporary collection.

It's a virtuous and vital cycle: more publicity means more curiosity and more curiosity means more publicity. And that means more art.

BEST LOCAL ART

> Fort Point Arts Community (p78)
> Gallery NAGA (p92)
> Mills Gallery at the Boston Center for the Arts (p107)
> Society of Arts & Crafts (p95)
> SoWa (p102)

BEST ART MUSEUMS

> Museum of Fine Arts (p110)
> ICA (p78)
> Isabella Stewart Gardner Museum (p110)
> List Center for Visual Arts (p118)
> Harvard Art Museum (p116)

MUSIC

'From Boston, Massachusetts, we are Morphine at your service.' So local rocker Mark Sandman would introduce his band when playing gigs around the country. From the supergroup Boston to the ska-core Mighty Mighty Bosstones, these bands like to be associated with their home-town. That's because this city has a tradition of grooving to great music.

Old-timers reminisce about the Ratskeller and the Channel, long gone and still sorely missed. But the rock scene still thrives around Boston, with dozens of stages in Allston, Cambridge and Somerville. Jazz venues are more limited, but the Berklee School of Music ensures a constant stream of new audiences and innovative performers.

There are several ways to get to know Boston's flourishing music scene. Firstly, hang out at Newbury Comics (p95 and p117). This Boston chain of record shops carries a great selection of CDs by local bands, keeping track of rising stars with its running list of top-sellers.

Secondly, visit **Band in Boston** (www.bandinbostonpodcast.com). Two local music fans make the rounds of area clubs, pick their favorite bands and broad-cast live performances from their living room in Somerville.

Finally, check out the local music festivals, including Blues Trust (p29) and Berklee Beantown Jazz Festival (p29). And festival or not, visit the music clubs around the city to hear Boston bands in their element.

BEST FOR ROCK
> Club Passim (p122)
> Church (p112)
> House of Blues (p113)
> Paradise Lounge (p113)

BEST FOR JAZZ & FOLK
> Beehive (p106)
> Lizard Lounge (p122)
> Wally's Café (p107)
> Regattabar (p122)

BEST FOR YOUR BOSTON PLAYLIST
> 'Let the Good Times Roll' – The Cars
> 'Start All Over' – J Geils Band
> 'Mass Ave' – Willie Alexander
> 'Do the Boob' – The Real Kids
> 'Bone Machine' – The Pixies
> 'Rascal King' – Mighty Mighty Bosstones
> 'Charlie on the MTA' – Kingston Trio
> 'No Place Like Home' – The Neighborhoods
> 'Tessie' – Dropkick Murphys
> 'Dirty Water' – The Standells

COMEDY

Boston is a funny place, and we mean funny ha-ha. Perhaps, as hypothesized by local comedian Jimmy Tingle (p44), it's true that Bostonians are twisted because their streets developed from cow paths. Or perhaps it's those weird accents that make everything sound so hilarious. Whatever the explanation, it's undeniable that Bostonians will crack you up.

To cite some famous examples: Conan O'Brien, Jay Leno, Stephen Wright, Denis Leary and Dane Cook are all Boston boys, not to mention funny females Andrea Martin and Amy Poehler. Many of these jokesters are graduates of Emerson College, which offers scholarships and workshops specifically devoted to comedy.

So when you are in Boston, where can you get a feel for the local funny bone? The most prestigious venue in town is the Wilbur Theatre (p89), which is the new home of the long-standing Comedy Connection. But there are many other options: improv groups performing in ratty theaters, wacky magicians making things disappear from a Chinese restaurant, hypnotists telling dirty jokes in the basement of a bar etc. There are dozens of these places tucked into tiny theaters and hidden theaters, especially in the Theater District.

And that is what is really exciting about Boston comedy – catching the funny people before they are famous…and laughing your head off.

If you want a concentrated dose of comedy, come for the **Boston Comedy Festival** (www.bostoncomedyfestival.com), which takes place during the first week in September.

Men in tights: Boston's comedic talent shows it has legs

FILM

Boston's demand for and production of independent film has blossomed in recent years. Suddenly, independent production companies are sprouting up around town, especially in the South End. Film festivals are all the rage, with local interest groups organizing events to showcase films catering to their people, be they bikies or bisexuals. Thanks to new legislation that gives tax breaks to moviemakers, the state of Massachusetts has become a prime location for filming, with Boston and Cambridge beginning to look like one big movie set.

The **Chlotrudis Society for Independent Film** (www.chlotrudis.org) is a local nonprofit organization that encourages thoughtful viewing of films. The idea is to promote film as an active and interactive art form, to encourage critique, discussion and feedback. The society offers a host of resources on its website.

Boston and its environs are home to several fine independent cinemas, but no Boston moviehouse is more beloved than the historic Brattle Theatre (p122). On the occasion of its 100th anniversary in 1990, one local journalist wrote that 'the Brattle Theatre…inspires a kind of nostalgia verging on worship.' In recent years, this longstanding cultural landmark has been under threat of closure due to lack of funding, but local film buffs rallied to raise the cash needed to sustain it.

BEST CINEMAS
> Brattle Theatre (p122)
> Somerville Theatre (p120)
> Museum of Fine Arts (p110)

BEST FILM FESTIVALS
> Independent Film Festival of Boston (p27; www.iffboston.org)
> Boston Underground Film Festival (www.bostonundergroundfilmfestival.org)
> Boston Bike Film Festival (www.bostonbikefilmfest.org)
> Boston Film Festival (www.bostonfilmfestival.org)

GLBT BOSTON

If you're queer and you're here, you can join the out-and-active gay communities that are visible all around Boston, especially in the South End and in Jamaica Plain. Pick up the weekly **Bay Windows** (www.baywindows.com) or stop by Calamus Bookstore (p84), both of which are excellent sources of information about community events and organizations.

No other organization has done so much for GLBT rights as **MassEquality** (☎ 617-878-2300; www.massequality.org). This impressive grassroots community was active in the success of gaining marriage equality in Massachusetts.

There is no shortage of entertainment options catering to GLBT travelers. From drag shows to dyke nights, this sexually diverse community has something for everybody. **Edge** (www.edgeboston.com) is an informative e-zine with lots of news, entertainment and commentary targeting gay audiences. **BGL Advertising Co** (www.bgladco.com) lists many gay and lesbian social and community groups, as well as entertainment venues and other general information.

The biggest event of the Boston gay and lesbian community is Boston Pride, a week of parades, parties, festivals and flag-raisings. See p27 for details.

BEST GLBT CLUBS & CAFÉS
> Club Café (p107)
> Diesel Cafe (p120)
> Estate (p89)
> Fritz (p106)

BEST PLACE TO EXPLORE YOUR INNER DIVA
> Jacques Cabaret (p89)

KIDS

Times were tough for kids in Boston back in the earliest days. In Puritan society, children were expected to obey, not play. There were a lot of chores, but few toys, as such diversions were considered distracting at best and sinful at worst.

The city has come a long way. Today Boston is filled with educational fun. Aside from obvious attractions such as the Museum of Science (p48), the New England Aquarium (p69) and, of course, the Children's Museum (p78), many adult-oriented museums and historic sites have special programs geared toward kids. So don't forget to think outside the box. Handy reference books include *Kidding Around Boston*, by Helen Byers, and Lonely Planet's *Travel With Children*.

Keep in mind that many services exist to make it easier to travel with children. Most sites and activities offer discounted rates for children, while the youngest tots often enjoy free admission. Hotels invite kids to stay free in the same room as their paying parents; restaurants offer half-portions and kids' menus. Families are a prime target market for the tourist industry in Boston, so most hotels, restaurants and tour services will do their best to accommodate the needs of you and your children.

BEST PARKS & PLAYGROUNDS
> Public Garden (p93)
> Boston Common (p58)
> Charles River Esplanade (p99)
> Back Bay Fens (p108)
> Castle Island (p78)

BEST KIDS' ACTIVITIES
> Family Place at the MFA (p110)
> Quacking it up on the Duck Tour (p166)
> Boston by Little Feet (p167)
> Wings over Boston at the Prudential Center Skywalk (p92)
> Exploring Fort Warren at Georges Island (p68)

BEST KIDS' EATING
> Bertucci's (p71)
> Flour (p80)
> Mr Bartley's Burger Cottage (p119)
> Quincy Market (p73)
> Zumes Coffee House (p45)

BEST KIDS' SHOPPING
> Curious George Goes to Wordsworth (p117)
> Red Wagon (p62)
> Pixie Stix (p61)

SCHOOL

The greater Boston area has many, many college campuses – and even more students. In summer this place can be hard to recognize, as the student haunts empty out and street parking frees up. But every fall, the city is transformed anew. U-Haul trucks block the streets and kids crowd the bars. From September to May, the city overflows with their exuberance. This renewable source of cultural energy supports sporting events, film festivals, music scenes, art galleries, coffee shops, hip clubs and Irish pubs. Many of these esteemed institutions offer opportunities for you to get in on it.

The most famous institutions are across the river in Cambridge: Harvard University (p116) and MIT (p118). West of Kenmore Sq, **Boston University** (www.bu.edu) has an enormous campus that includes the excellent archives at Mugar Memorial Library. The **University of Massachusetts, Boston** (UMass; www.umb.edu) hosts the John F Kennedy Library & Museum (p78).

The country's first public art school, **Massachusetts College of Art** (MassArt; www.massart.edu) offers constantly rotating exhibits, while the **Berklee College of Music** (www.berklee.edu) is one of the country's finest music schools, often putting on recitals by students and alum.

Boston College (www.bc.edu) is home to the nation's largest Jesuit community. The leafy green campus on the edge of town has Gothic towers, stained glass, a good art museum and excellent Irish and Catholic ephemera collections in the library. Its basketball and football teams are usually high in the national rankings.

In the western suburbs, **Wellesley College** (www.wellesley.edu) is a Seven Sisters women's college that has a hilly, wooded campus and the excellent Davis Museum & Cultural Center.

Much revered, Harvard University is at the center of Cambridge's cultural energy (p116)

SCIENCE

We hear a lot about the arts in Boston, but what about the science? After all, this city is home to the Massachusetts Institute of Technology (p118), which is a sort of scientific superpower among universities.

The technology and biotechnology industries spawned from university research labs (quite literally, as MIT researchers developed the first computer in 1928). Wang Computers, Digital Computers, Prime and Data General all began in the Boston area. It was even an MIT computer scientist – one JCR Licklider – who first conceived of a 'galactic network,' an idea which would later spawn the internet.

Cambridge – especially Central and Kendall Sqs – is also a center for the pharmaceutical industry, hosting companies such as Millennium and Biogen.

The hospitals form collaborative relationships with universities for teaching and research. The world-class facilities at the Longwood Medical Area and Massachusetts General Hospital are affiliated with Harvard Medical School, while the New England Medical Center maintains a relationship with Tufts University. Boston institutions receive more funding than those in any other urban area from the National Institute for Health.

Are you blinded yet?

BEST GEEKY FUN
> Museum of Science (p48)
> New England Aquarium (p69)
> MIT Museum (p118)
> Harvard Museum of Natural History (p116)

BEST FOR DOING YOUR MATH HOMEWORK
> Boston Public Library (p92)
> Algiers Coffee House (p119)
> Zumes Coffee House (p45)
> Courtyard of the Isabella Stewart Gardner Museum (p110)
> Other Side Cosmic Café (p111)

V

SNAPSHOTS

SHOPPING

This town is known for its intellect and its arts, so you can bet it's good for bookstores, art galleries and music shops. But these days, the streets of Boston and Cambridge are also sprinkled with offbeat and independent boutiques – many carrying the latest styles from New York, but many also carrying up-and-coming local designers. Besides to-die-for duds, indie shops hawk handmade jewelry, exotic household decorations and arty quirky gifts. These are the kind of places that are fun to browse, even if you don't intend to buy.

Except on rare occasions, these unique and fashionable shops will not thrill bargain-hunters, but the Boston institution Filene's Basement will (see p70). Thrifty shoppers will find more than enough factory outlets and secondhand shops to test their pay-off-the-credit-card resolve.

If you intend to engage in a little shop therapy, you have several options. Back Bay (p93) is the traditional 'shopping and lunch' destination, its streets lined with boutiques and galleries. But both the South End (p102) and the North End (p48) are emerging as shopping destinations, as creative entrepreneurs open shops and galleries alongside the restaurants that these neighborhoods are better known for.

Others may prefer the hustle and bustle of Downtown Crossing (p70), where large department stores and smaller practical retail outlets cater to everyday Bostonians.

Beacon Hill (p60) is the traditional spot for antiquing, although Charles St is also home to cutesy boutiques, fancy galleries and neighborhood shops. In Cambridge, Harvard Sq (p117) has always been famous for its used bookstores and secondhand record shops.

BEST FOR GIFTS
> Beacon Hill Chocolates (p60)
> Motley (p102)
> Shake the Tree (p49)
> WardMaps (p118)

BEST FOR STUFF MADE IN BOSTON
> Aunt Sadie's Candlestix (p102)
> Cibeline (p60)
> Jake's House (p94)
> Local Charm (p71)
> North Bennet Street School (p49)
> Oak (p95)
> South End Open Market (p103)

SPORTS

Boston puts the 'fanatic' in sports fan. And why not, with the three-time world champion New England Patriots, the long-overdue World Series–winning Red Sox and the most recent NBA champion Celtics?

Emotions run especially high around baseball. The intensity of baseball fans has only increased since the **Boston Red Sox** (www.redsox.com) broke their agonizing 86-year losing streak and won the 2004 World Series. The Old Town Team repeated their feat in 2007 and came awfully close in 2008, which means they continue to sell out every game. Get a taste of the passion by logging on to **SOSH** (www.sonsofsamhorn.com).

Sports fanaticism is not limited to baseball. This is evident from the face painters and beer bellies that brave subzero temperatures to watch the **Patriots** (www.patriots.com) play football. The Pats were Super Bowl champions in 2002, 2004 and 2005 – that's a 'three-peat' for football fans. But supporters had their hearts broken in 2007, when they ruined their perfect season by losing the Super Bowl. New England fans are still recovering.

The **Boston Celtics** (www.celtics.com) have won more basketball championships than any other NBA team. Most of these victories occurred back in the 1980s, when the team was led by basketball legend Larry Bird. After a 22-year dry spell, the Celtics surprised the city in 2008 with an NBA championship.

Even hockey fans were cheering at the time of research, as the **Bruins** (www.bostonbruins.com) lead their division of the NHL. In 2008, the *Sporting News* voted Boston 'the best sports city in America.' As if Bostonians needed outside confirmation that they live in the City of Champions.

'Take me out to the ball game': the Red Sox get ready to play at Fenway Park (p112)

V

THEATER & DANCE

Boston's Puritan roots have always exercised a stranglehold over her desire to become a world-class city, and this clash is most apparent in the city's stunted theater tradition. Throughout the 20th century, Boston's high-handed morality made it the butt of many jokes, as savvy marketing moguls designated their productions 'banned in Boston' and were therefore guaranteed a full house elsewhere. Only in recent years has the city developed as a destination for interesting alternative theatrical productions, most of which take place at the Boston Center for the Arts (p107). See www.bostontheaterscene.com for programming info. Other excellent theater companies include the American Repertory Theater (p122) and the Huntington Theatre Company (p113).

Boston stages play the role of testing ground for major musicals before they head to Broadway. Several of the gilded venues in the Theater District participate in **Broadway Across America** (www.broadwayacrossamerica.com), which allows spectators across the country to see the best of New York theater.

Boston's preeminent dance company is the **Boston Ballet** (www.bostonballet .com), founded by E Virginia Williams in 1965. That December, Arthur Fiedler conducted the first two performances of *The Nutcracker*, which would become a Boston tradition. The Boston Ballet normally performs at the Opera House (p75).

So you think you can dance? **Swing** (www.havetodance.com) and **Salsa** (www .salsaboston.com) attract lively followings. The **Boston Dance Alliance** (www.boston dancealliance.org) is another excellent resource.

Half-price tickets are available on the day of performance at **BosTix** (www .bostix.com), with kiosks on Copley Sq and near Faneuil Hall.

BEST FOR TANTALIZING THEATER

> American Repertory Theater (p122)
> Speakeasy Stage Company (www .speakeasystage.com)
> Pilgrim Theatre (www.pilgrim theatre.org)
> Company One (www.companyone.org)
> The Theater Offensive (www.the theateroffensive.org)

BEST FOR DARING DANCE

> Snappy Dance Theater (www.snappy dance.com)
> Bennett Dance Company (www .bennettdancecompany.org)
> Lostwax (www.lostwax.com)
> Zoé Dance (www.zoedance.org)

RAPHAEL
TITIAN
REMBRANDT
VELASQUEZ

PHIDIAS
PRAXITELES
MICHELANGELO
DONATELLO

Outside the Boston Public Library (p92)

BACKGROUND

HISTORY

CITY ON A HILL

The first trickle of immigrants arrived in New England in 1620, when the Pilgrims established a small colony in Plymouth (see p127). Ten years later, the flagship *Arbella* led a flotilla of a thousand Puritans on the treacherous transatlantic crossing. Upon arrival, country squire John Winthrop gazed out on the Shawmut Peninsula and declared, 'we shall be as a City upon a Hill, with the eyes of all people upon us.'

The founders of the Massachusetts Bay Colony sought to build 'a model of Christian clarity,' where personal virtue and industry replaced the smug class hierarchy and decadence of aristocratic England. To ensure the colony's decent development, the new settlement was governed by a spiritual elite – a Puritan theocracy – and the Church dominated early colonial life.

The Puritans also valued education. To promote literacy, they established America's first public school (on the site of Old City Hall) and public library. In 1636, Harvard College (p116) was founded to supply the colony with homegrown enlightened ministers. These institutions established early on Boston's reputation as an intellectual hub.

CRADLE OF LIBERTY

In the mid-18th century, Britain became entangled in some expensive wars. Covetous of New England's maritime wealth, the Crown instituted a series of tariffs, restricting and taxing colonial trade. New England merchants protested, citing the principle of 'no taxation without representation.' Tensions mounted, as the Sons of Liberty, a clandestine network of patriots, stirred up resistance to British policy.

In March 1770 a motley street gang provoked British regulars with slurs and snowballs until the troops fired into the crowd, killing five people. John Adams successfully defended the British troops in court, but the Sons of Liberty scored a propaganda coup with their depictions of the Boston Massacre (see p70).

Three years later, the Tea Act incited further destruction. Protesters boarded three merchant ships and dumped 90,000 pounds of taxable tea into the harbor. The British response to the Boston Tea Party was harsh: the port was blockaded and the city placed under military rule. Angry citizens began organizing themselves into 'Minutemen' militia groups.

The conflict finally came to a head when British troops marched west to Concord to seize a hidden stash of gunpowder. The sexton at the Old North Church (p48) hung two lanterns in the steeple to signal the troop movement, and Paul Revere quietly galloped into the night to alert the Minutemen. At daybreak, the Redcoats skirmished with Minutemen on the Lexington Green (p125) and the Old North Bridge in Concord (p125). So started the War for Independence.

Boston figured prominently in the early phase of the American Revolution, especially the 1775 Battle of Bunker Hill (p42). Finally, on March 17, 1776, the British evacuated and Boston was liberated.

ATHENS OF AMERICA

After independence, Boston entered a commercial and cultural boom. By the middle of the 19th century, steam power and manufacturing shifted the economy and spurred another revolution – the industrial revolution.

Industrial wealth transformed Boston. The tops of hills were used for landfill to expand its size, creating the French-style Back Bay, while Frederick Law Olmsted designed the Emerald Necklace (p113). The city established cultural institutions including the Museum of Fine Arts (p110), the Boston Symphony Orchestra (p112) and the Boston Public Library (p92).

Boston emerged as a center of enlightenment in the young republic. The city's second mayor, Josiah Quincy, led an effort to remake the city's underclass into industrious and responsible citizens, expanding public education. Influenced by an idealistic legacy, Boston gave rise to the first uniquely American intellectual movement, transcendentalism, led by Ralph Waldo Emerson. Bostonians were at the forefront of progressive movements such as abolitionism and suffrage. Besides philosophy, the city became a vibrant cultural center for poetry, painting, architecture, science and scholarship, earning Boston the reputation as the Athens of America.

MODERN BOSTON

The rapid rise of industry led to social change. The city was inundated with an influx of immigrants: the Boston Brahmin (a collective name for Boston's leading families) was forced to mix with the Irish working class, Old World Italians and Portuguese fisherfolk.

Anti-immigrant and anti-Catholic sentiments were shrill. Nonetheless, Brahmin dominance of Boston politics slipped away. The Democratic Party became the political instrument of the working poor, featuring flamboyant populist politicians such as Mayor James Michael Curley.

Two of the city's oldest neighborhoods – Scollay Sq and the West End – were destroyed by 'urban renewal,' resulting in the controversial new City Hall Plaza. But eventually, modern Boston came to embody the old and the new, a coexistence of red brick with steel and glass.

With the decline of manufacturing in the 20th century, the economy faltered and Boston had to remake itself yet again. Thanks to the formidable presence of the universities, the city developed into a center for high-tech industries, medicine and financial services.

Since the beginning, Boston has been a champion of civil rights and social reform. In the 21st century, Boston again became a battle site, this time for gay and lesbian rights. In 2004, by order of the state supreme court, the country's first legal gay marriage took place in Cambridge. Meanwhile, in the state capitol – in anticipation of Obama-mania – Massachusetts elected Harvard grad Deval Patrick, the state's first African American governor and the country's second.

Although Boston is famous for its ties to history, the city continues to see itself on the frontlines of progress. As the challenges of the 21st century unfold, Boston moves forward while drawing on its past.

LIFE AS A BOSTONIAN

Bostonians are culture vultures. Whether it's Stravinsky's *Symphony of Psalms* performed by the Boston Symphony Orchestra or *I Will Survive* performed by a drag-queen version of Gloria Gaynor, Boston is into creating and consuming art of every variety.

Bostonians are also sports fans. Sure, almost everybody loves to watch the Sox; but Bostonians also recognize that life is not a spectator sport. They are just as likely to be playing on the company softball team as watching the boys on TV. Pick a sport and Boston has an intramural league; find an open space and you'll see someone throwing a Frisbee. Bike paths, basketball courts, boathouses and beaches are always in use by Boston's young, energetic population.

Bostonians are liberal thinkers. At least that's what the numbers say: the city votes Democratic in elections on almost every level. While the reality is always more complex than the numbers, Boston has emerged ahead of the pack on issues from gay marriage to universal healthcare.

Bostonians are education addicts. Perhaps there is something in the water – and perhaps the local universities and colleges put it there – but residents of Boston have an unquenchable thirst for learning at all ages.

The Cambridge Center for Adult Education is the country's oldest community education program, while Boston has a similar lineup. Many local institutions – including Harvard, BU and Northeastern – have 'continuing education' programs for nondegree-seeking students. Whether it's belly dancing, poetry or astronomy, classes cater to curious folks who seek to develop new skills and interests.

ART & ARCHITECTURE

Shortly after the American Revolution, Boston set to work building its new city, and Charles Bulfinch took responsibility for much of it, creating Faneuil Hall (p68) and the Massachusetts State House (p58), as well as private homes for Boston's most distinguished citizens.

As the city expanded in the late 19th century, so did the opportunities for creative art and architecture, especially with the new construction in the Back Bay. Frederick Law Olmsted designed the Charles River Esplanade (p99) and the Emerald Necklace (p113), two magnificent green spaces that snake around the city. Copley Sq represents the pinnacle of 19th-century architecture. Henry Hobson Richardson's Trinity Church (p93), with its heavy massing and subdued towers, directly fronts McKim, Mead and White's Boston Public Library (p92), a Renaissance Revival masterpiece modeled after an Italian Renaissance palazzo. During this period, Boston's most celebrated artist was John Singer Sargent (1856–1925), whose murals adorn the central staircase at the Museum of Fine Arts (p110) and the walls of the Boston Public Library (p92).

Also from this period, Daniel Chester French (1850–1931) was the creator of the Minuteman statue in Concord (p125) and the John Harvard statue in Harvard Yard (p116), not to mention better-known works in Washington, DC. Augustus St Gaudens (1848–1907) is famous for the Robert Gould Shaw Memorial on the Boston Common (p58), but he was also a key figure in the design of the Boston Public Library, where his work is on display.

The 20th century witnessed plenty of noteworthy additions. IM Pei is responsible for the much-hated City Hall Plaza and the much beloved John F Kennedy Library (p78). His partner James Cobb designed the stunning John Hancock Tower.

Critics claim that Boston lost pace with the artistic world in the second half of the 20th century. But the visual arts have returned to the forefront of contemporary cultural life in the new millennium. Several new buildings on the MIT campus have made industrial East Cambridge the city's most daring neighborhood for design. Meanwhile, the dramatic new space for the Institute of Contemporary Art (p78) has shined the spotlight onto Boston's long-overshadowed contemporary art scene. Even the Museum of Fine Arts has stepped up to the challenge, investing in a long-term upgrade to its contemporary collection.

GOVERNMENT & POLITICS

The late Thomas P 'Tip' O'Neill, Boston native and respected Speaker of the House, coined the phrase 'All politics is local.' So for example, if the mayor can keep control of the day-to-day practicalities of the functioning of the city, he's 'in like Flynn' (the long-serving Irish mayor Ray Flynn, that is).

Boston's current chief is Thomas Menino, the city's first Italian-American mayor (and first non-Irish mayor since 1884). Fondly called 'Mumbles Menino' for his poor diction, Menino is nonetheless well liked due to his hands-on approach to managing the city. By the time he completes his current, fourth term in office in 2009, he will be the longest-serving mayor in Boston history.

Despite Menino's positive standing, the city administration faces criticism on several fronts. The lack of affordable housing is a huge issue, as neighborhood gentrification has driven up real-estate prices. With the economy in recession at the time of writing, the city was facing a major budget shortfall and the mayor was threatening to lay off as many as 700 employees. At the time of research, Boston was buzzing as Menino had finally announced that he would seek a fifth term in office in the 2009 election.

Even if Tip O'Neill was right, Boston continues to play an important role in national politics. The city provided candidates for two recent presidential campaigns (Democrat John Kerry in 2004 and Republican Mitt Romney in 2008) although – obviously – neither bid was successful.

Boston is often considered the epitome of the 'liberal East Coast.' And it's true that the city strongly supports Democratic candidates. Massachusetts has been at the forefront of countless 'liberal' issues, including anti-smoking legislation (Massachusetts banned smoking in the workplace in 2003), same-sex marriage (legalized in Massachusetts in 2004) and healthcare (as of 2007, health insurance is required for all state residents and subsidized for low-income residents).

ENVIRONMENT

Bostonians have the great fortune to witness the greening of their city, quite literally. The Central Artery, now underground and out of sight, has been replaced by the Rose Kennedy Greenway. This new park provides a pleasant counterpart to the Charles River Esplanade on the south shore of the river, and the Emerald Necklace, which stretches from the Boston Common to Franklin Park. And certainly after 15 years of Big Dig construction, the greenway is a welcome addition to an otherwise concrete landscape.

Other ongoing environmental initiatives are also coming to fruition. For hundreds of years, the Boston Harbor was a dumping site for sewage, earning its reputation as the most polluted waterfront in the country. In the mid-1980s, the city was ordered by the Environmental Protection Agency (EPA) to clean up its act. The long-term effort has finally reaped benefits. For the first time in over a century, water quality in the harbor is safe for swimming; beaches are clean and enjoyable places to play; and the waterfront has become a wonderful area for strolling.

A similar effort is underway in the Charles River, inspiration for the Standell's song *Dirty Water*. Improvements have been significant. In 2008 the Charles River Initiative received its highest grade ever on its report card from the EPA. This B++ is a vast improvement on the D it received a decade ago, though nobody anticipates that the Charles River beaches will open any time soon.

Another green goal in Boston is reducing the number of cars on the roads, thus diminishing greenhouse gas emissions. Boston-based Zipcar – the country's largest car-sharing company – encourages urbanites to shed cars, drive less and use other forms of transportation. This trend complements the city's long-term transportation plans to extend the subway and build more bike paths ('long-term' being the operative word).

The City of Boston has undertaken other eco-friendly initiatives, hiring its first 'sustainability officer' in 2008. Programs under investigation include installing solar-powered parking meters, requiring cabbies to drive hybrid vehicles, conducting energy audits of public buildings and hiring green janitorial services.

FURTHER READING

FICTION

Nathaniel Hawthorne wrote *The Scarlet Letter* (1850) about a woman in Puritan New England who is vilified when she becomes pregnant with her minister's child. Hawthorne was apparently inspired by the gravestone of Elizabeth Pain, in King's Chapel Burial Ground, for his protagonist Hester Prynne.

Henry James wrote several novels set in Boston, including the aptly named *The Bostonians* (1886). A Boston feminist takes her conservative male cousin to hear a speech by a rising star of the women's movement. They both fall in love with her, resulting in a tragicomic love triangle.

Edwin O'Connor's *The Last Hurrah* (1955), a fictional work based on Mayor Curley's antics, is as much fun as Jack Beatty's *The Rascal King* (1992), a biographical account of Curley's flamboyance.

David Foster Wallace's *Infinite Jest* (1996) includes intricate descriptions of Commonwealth Ave, Back Bay and the Boston Common. The 1000-page tome is at once philosophical and satirical, and earned Wallace the MacArthur Genius Award.

Born and raised in Dorchester, Dennis Lehane wrote *Mystic River* (2001) and *Gone Baby Gone* (1998), both compelling tales set in working-class Boston 'hoods, both of which were made into acclaimed films.

By contrast, Jhumpa Lahiri represents the 'new' Boston. She is a Bengali Indian American writer who studied creative writing at Boston University, and some of her books are set here. A book of short stories, *Interpreter of Maladies* (1999) won the Pulitzer Prize for fiction, while her follow-up novella *The Namesake* (2003) was made into a film. Both books address the challenges and triumphs in the lives of her Indian American characters.

NONFICTION

There is no shortage of riveting books about every aspect of Boston's history. For a taste of the Puritan lifestyle and an introduction to America's 'founding mother' read *American Jezebel*, Eve LaPlante's excellent biography of the martyr Anne Hutchinson.

David Hackett Fischer gives a suspenseful account of Boston's patriots and the events that started a revolution in *Paul Revere's Ride*, while Russell Duncan's *Where Death Meets Glory* is a personalized take on Robert Gould Shaw and the 54th Regiment of black soldiers and their heroically tragic campaign.

In *Dark Tide*, Stephen Puleo tells the suspenseful and sorrowful tale of the 1919 Molasses Disaster in the North End, when a molasses tank exploded and killed 21 people.

For an equally dark story from contemporary times, read *Black Mass: The True Story of an Unholy Alliance between the FBI and the Irish Mob*. Dick Lehr and Gerard O'Neill give the dope on local hood Whitey Bulger and why he is on the lam, instead of in the slammer.

FILMS

In recent years, the state of Massachusetts started offering tax incentives for film production companies, making Boston a major destination for moviemakers. (Unfortunately, the state cannot guarantee the quality of the films.)

That said, 2007 was a very good year for Boston in film. Matt Damon costarred with Leonardo DiCaprio in *The Departed,* which takes place in Boston. This suspense-filled mob movie won Best Picture. Based on the novel by Dennis Lehane, *Gone Baby Gone* was another thriller that was also nominated for an Oscar.

That was the second successful film based on a Lehane novel, the first being *Mystic River* (2006), which earned Academy Awards for Sean Penn and Tim Robbins. It's the dark story of three childhood friends who are thrown together in adulthood when one of their daughters is murdered.

A few films in the 1990s showed off Boston's colorful neighborhoods. The art-house hit *Next Stop Wonderland* (1997), a heartwarming independent film about a young woman's dating travails, refers to the final T stop on the blue line. *Good Will Hunting* (1997) put Southie on the Hollywood map and started the careers of Cambridge boys Matt Damon and Ben Affleck.

Not surprisingly, Boston and its environs have been the setting for several noteworthy historical films. *Amistad* (1997), with an all-star cast directed by Steven Spielberg, tells the true story of a mutiny aboard a slave ship and the ensuing legal battle to vindicate the mutineers. *The Crucible* (1996), with Daniel Day-Lewis and Winona Ryder, is a film adaptation of Arthur Miller's play about the 1692 Salem witch trials.

Little Women (1994) is based on Louisa May Alcott's wonderful book about sisters growing up in 19th-century Concord. The chick flick stars Susan Sarandon as Marmie and Winona Ryder as Jo. *Glory* (1989), starring Denzel Washington and Matthew Broderick, tells the true story of the first Civil War black volunteer infantry unit.

There are a few oldies but goodies, which some claim are still the best (and most authentic) Boston movies. In *The Verdict* (1982), Paul Newman plays a Boston lawyer who takes on a medical malpractice case. The original *Thomas Crown Affair* (1968), starring Steve McQueen and Faye Dunaway, depicts the city as the perfect place to stage the perfect crime. Speaking of which, director William Friedkin of *The Brink's Job* (1978) insisted on authentic North End locations and hired local ex-cons to play toughs.

DIRECTORY

TRANSPORTATION
ARRIVAL & DEPARTURE

AIR

Logan International Airport

On MA 1A in East Boston, **Logan International Airport** (☎ 800-235-6426; www.massport.com) has five separate terminals that are connected by a frequent shuttle bus (bus 11). Public information booths are located in the baggage claim areas of each terminal.

Manchester Airport

A quiet alternative to Logan, **Manchester Airport** (☎ 603-624-6556; www.flymanchester.com) is just 55 miles north of Boston in New Hampshire.

Flight Line, Inc (☎ 800-245-2525; www.flightlineinc.com) operates a shuttle from Manchester airport to the orange-line Sullivan Sq T station in Charlestown for $19 per person. Reservations required.

TF Green Airport

Just outside the city of Providence (Rhode Island), **TF Green Airport** (☎ 401-737-4000; www.pvdairport.com) is also serviced by major carriers. The airport is one hour south of Boston.

The **MBTA commuter rail** (www.mbta .com) offers regular service from South Station to downtown Providence ($7.75, one hour). The service is supposed to be extended to TF Green Airport in 2010. In the meantime, there is an airport shuttle that plies this route.

TRAIN

The national railway line is **Amtrak** (☎ 800-872-7245; www.amtrak.com; 🚇 South Station). Trains leave from South Station, located at Atlantic Ave and Summer St; the trains also stop at Back Bay Station at Dartmouth St. Trains travel frequently down the East Cost to New York

CLIMATE CHANGE & TRAVEL

Travel – especially air travel – is a significant contributor to global climate change. At Lonely Planet, we believe that all travelers have a responsibility to limit their personal impact. As a result, we have teamed with Rough Guides and other concerned industry partners to support Climate Care, which allows travelers to offset the greenhouse gases they are responsible for with contributions to energy-saving projects and other climate-friendly initiatives in the developing world. Lonely Planet offsets all staff and author travel.

For more information, turn to the responsible travel pages on lonelyplanet.com. For details on offsetting your carbon emissions and a carbon calculator, go to www.climate care.org.

Travel to/from the Airport

	Taxi	T (Subway)	T (Silver Line Bus)	Water Taxi
Pick-up Point	All terminals	Airport T station	All terminals	Logan dock
Drop-off Point	Anywhere	Downtown (Aquarium, State or Government Center T stations)	Seaport District or South Station	Long Wharf or Rowes Wharf
Duration	20min to center	20min	20min	20min
Cost	$30 to center	$1.70-2	$1.70-$2	round-trip $10/17
Other	n/a	🕐 5:30am-12:30am	🕐 5:30am-12:30am	🕐 7am-10pm Mon-Sat, 8am-8pm Sun
Contact	www.planet tran.com	www.mbta.com	www.mbta.com	www.citywatertaxi.com, www.roweswharfwater taxi.com

and Washington, DC. The service to New York City's Penn Station costs $89 one-way and takes four to 4½ hours. The high-speed Acela service to Manhattan (three to 3½ hours) is more expensive ($109 to $140 one-way); reservations are required. Amtrak's online 'Rail Sale' program offers substantial discounts on many reserved tickets.

VISA

Getting into the United States can be a bureaucratic nightmare, depending on your country of origin. For up-to-date information about visas and immigration, check with the **US State Department** (www.unitedstatesvisas.gov).

Most foreign visitors to the US need a visa. However, there is a Visa Waiver Program through which citizens of certain countries may enter the US without a visa for stays of 90 days or less, providing they have an e-passport. This list is subject to continual re-examination and bureaucratic finagling, but includes: Andorra, Australia, Austria, Belgium, Brunei, Denmark, Finland, France, Germany, Iceland, Ireland, Italy, Japan, Liechtenstein, Luxembourg, Monaco, the Netherlands, New Zealand, Norway, Portugal, San Marino, Singapore, Slovenia, Spain, Sweden, Switzerland and the UK. It was recently expanded to include the

Czech Republic, Estonia, Hungary, Latvia, Lithuania, Malta, Slovakia and South Korea.

Under this program, you must have a round-trip ticket or ticket to any onward foreign destination and you will not be allowed to extend your stay beyond 90 days.

GETTING AROUND

While Boston is a walking city, you will want to use the subway (the T), the bus or the commuter rail to reach some destinations. In this book, the nearest T station is noted after the 🚇 icon in each listing.

TRAVEL PASSES

Tourist passes with unlimited travel (on subway, bus or water shuttle) are available for periods of one week ($15) and one day ($9). Kids aged five to 11 ride for free. Passes may be purchased at the following T stations: Park St, Government Center, Back Bay, Alewife, Copley, Quincy Adams, Harvard, North Station, South Station, Hynes and Airport.

SUBWAY (THE T)

The **MBTA** (☎ 617-222-3200, 800-392-6100; www.mbta.com) operates the USA's oldest subway, known locally as the 'T.' There are four lines – red, blue, green and orange – that radiate from the principal downtown stations: Park St, Downtown Crossing, Government Center and State.

NO-FLY ZONE

Air travel is the worst form of transportation for emitting greenhouse gases (or best, if your goal is to give off as much carbon dioxide as possible). It should come as no surprise that your ability to avoid air travel to Boston will be directly related to your place of origin.

The good news is that if you are coming from the East Coast, there is no shortage of overland routes. Buses and trains run up and down the Eastern Seaboard, connecting the cities from Washington, DC to New York to Boston.

Even if you are coming from other parts of the country, you might travel overland if you have some time to spare. (Trans-Continental Railroad, anyone?) Driving offers an opportunity to see and experience the countryside along the way. Companies such as **Auto Driveaway** (www.autodriveaway.com) can hook you up with a car that needs a driver to your destination.

Intercontinental travelers will have a tougher time of it, of course. Unless you were thinking of taking a transatlantic cruise.

In any case, once you're in Boston get around town by walking, biking or taking the T. Never mind the driving woes and parking tickets; you'll also reduce carbon emissions. It's a win-win-win.

Travel Times in Boston

	Faneuil Hall	Park St	Copley Sq	Kenmore Sq	Harvard Sq
Faneuil Hall	n/a	walk 10min	T 10min	T 25min	T 30min
Park St	walk 10min	n/a	walk 20min	T 20min	T 20min
Copley Sq	T 10min	walk 20min	n/a	walk 20min	T 30min
Kenmore Sq	T 25min	T 20min	walk 20min	n/a	T 40min
Harvard Sq	T 30min	T 20min	T 30min	T 40min	n/a

When traveling away from any of these stations, you are heading outbound.

Buy a paper ticket ($2 per ride) from the machines in any terminal. Better yet, request a plastic Charlie Card ($1.70 per ride) from an attendant and use the machines to add as much money as you think you will need. In either case, the terminal will read your ticket or card and deduct the fare as you pass through.

The T operates services from approximately 5:30am to 12:30am. The last red line trains pass through Park St at about 12:30am (depending on the direction), but all T stations and lines are different.

BUS

The **MBTA** (☎ 617-222-5215; www.mbta .com) operates bus routes within the city. These can be difficult to figure out for the short-term visitor, but schedules are posted on its website and at some bus stops along the routes. The standard bus fare is $1.50, or $1.25 with a Charlie Card. If you're transferring from the T on a Charlie Card the bus fare is free.

The Silver Line, a so-called 'rapid' bus, starts at Downtown Crossing and runs along Washington St in the South End to Roxbury's Dudley Sq. Another route goes from South Station to the Seaport District, then under the harbor to Logan International Airport. This waterfront route costs $2 ($1.70 with a Charlie Card), instead of the normal fare.

BOAT

Boston Harbor Cruises (Map p67; ☎ 617-227-4321; www.bostonharborcruises; Long Wharf; adult/child $1.70/0.85; ⏱ 6:30am-8pm Mon-Fri, 10am-6pm Sat & Sun; 🚇 Aquarium) Operates a commuter service to Charlestown Navy Yard.

City Water Taxi (Map p67; ☎ 617-422-0392; www.citywatertaxi.com; fare $10; ⏱ 7am-

10pm Mon-Sat, to 8pm Sun) Makes on-demand taxi stops at about 15 waterfront points.

TRAIN

The **MBTA commuter rail** (☎ 617-222-3200, 800-392-6100; www.mbta.com) operates services to destinations in the metropolitan Boston area. Trains heading west and north of the city, including to Concord and Salem, leave from bustling North Station on Causeway St. Trains heading south, including to Plymouth, leave from South Station.

TAXI

Cabs are plentiful but expensive. Rates are determined by the meter, which calculates miles. Expect to pay about $10 to $20 between most tourist points within the city limits, without much traffic. Recommended taxi companies include **Top Cab** (☎ 617-266-4800) and **Chill Out First Class Cab** (☎ 617-212-3763) in Cambridge.

PRACTICALITIES

BUSINESS HOURS

For the purposes of this book, hours are included in the reviews only where they do not conform to the following norm.

Banks are open from 8:30am to 4pm Monday through Friday. Some banks are open until 6pm on Friday and also from 9am to noon on Saturday. Businesses are open from 9am to 5pm Monday through Friday.

Bars and clubs are open till midnight daily, and often stay open till 1am or 2am on Friday and Saturday nights.

Restaurants start serving at 11am or 11:30am daily and close at 9pm or 10pm. Restaurants serving breakfast open from 6am or 7am to 10am. Some places will close from 2:30pm or 3pm and reopen at 5:30pm for dinner.

Shops open at 9am or 10am and close at 6pm or 7pm, Monday to Saturday; some also open from noon to 5pm on Sundays. Major shopping areas and malls keep extended hours.

HOLIDAYS

New Year's Day January 1
Martin Luther King Jr's Birthday January – third Monday
Presidents' Day February – third Monday
Evacuation Day March 17
Patriots' Day April – third Monday
Memorial Day May – last Monday
Independence Day July 4
Labor Day September – first Monday
Columbus Day October – second Monday
Veterans Day November 11
Thanksgiving Day November – fourth Thursday
Christmas Day December 25

INTERNET

INTERNET ACCESS

Most hotels and hostels offer internet access in one way or another.

It usually means wireless access, though some hotels also have an on-site business center or internet corner that provides computers.

Wireless access is also free at many restaurants and cafés, including Cask 'n Flagon (p112), Sonsie (p98) and Trident Booksellers & Café (p98). Look for the 💻 icon in the listings. For a long list of wi-fi locations around the city, see www.wi-fihotspotlist.com.

The city of Boston is implementing a plan called **Main Streets Wifi** (www.mainstreetswifi.com), with a goal of using wireless technology to bridge the digital divide. The plan is to install a citywide wireless network. The project started right downtown, with one hot spot at Faneuil Hall (p68) and City Hall Plaza and another covering Christopher Columbus Park and Long Wharf. Other access points are in Roslindale, Washington Gateway and other underserved communities.

INTERNET RESOURCES

Blogs, chats and other internet randomness for your entertainment and edification:

Boston (www.bostonusa.com) The official website of the Greater Boston Convention & Visitors Bureau.

Boston Blogs (www.bostonblogs.com) Links to more than 1000 blogs about various aspects of Beantown life.

Boston Central (www.bostoncentral.com) A fantastic resource for families, with listings for activities, outings, shopping and restaurants that are good for kids.

Boston Globe (www.boston.com) The online presence of the *Boston Globe*, with up-to-date weather, blog posts and extensive entertainment listings.

Boston Independent Media Center (www.boston.indymedia.org) An alternative voice for local news and events.

Boston Online (www.boston-online.com) Source of valuable info such as public restroom reviews and an English-Bostonese glossary.

DogBoston (www.dogboston.com) Everything man's best friend needs to know about Boston.

Sons of Sam Horn (www.sonsofsamhorn.com) Dedicated to discussion of all things Red Sox. Curt Schilling has been known to occasionally post.

Universal Hub (www.universalhub.com) Bostonians talk to each other about whatever is on their mind (sometimes nothing).

MONEY

EXCHANGE RATES

Prices in this book are quoted in United States dollars (US$). US$1=100 cents. For current exchange rates see www.xe.com.

Australia	A$1	$0.74
Canada	C$1	$0.85
Euro zone	€1	$1.34
Hong Kong	HK$1	$0.13
Japan	¥100	$1.01
New Zealand	NZ$1	$0.58
Singapore	S$1	$0.68
Switzerland	Sfr1	$0.89
UK	UK£1	$1.50

COSTS

Boston is an expensive place to visit. Three sit-down meals a day, including one at an upscale restaurant, will easily cost $60 per person. At best, self-catering and cheap eats make it possible to eat for about $20 per day. Most museums charge $12 to $20 for adults, usually half-price for children.

Keep in mind that Boston offers many opportunities to save money, including sights, activities and entertainment options that are free of charge. Students and seniors often get reduced rates with a valid ID, while children may be admitted free of charge, depending on their age.

NEWSPAPERS & MAGAZINES

Bay Windows (www.baywindows.com) Serves the gay and lesbian community.
Boston Globe (www.boston.com) One of two major daily newspapers; publishes an extensive calendar section every Thursday and the daily Sidekick, both of which include entertainment options.
Boston Herald (www.bostonherald.com) The more right-wing daily, competing with the *Globe*; has its own Scene section published every Friday.
Boston Magazine (www.bostonmagazine .com) The city's monthly glossy magazine.
Boston Phoenix (www.bostonphoenix.com) The 'alternative' paper that focuses on arts and entertainment; published weekly.

Improper Bostonian (www.improper.com) A sassy biweekly distributed free from sidewalk dispenser boxes.
Lola (www.lolaboston.com) 'Boston's new best friend' is like a women's magazine with a local focus. Includes local bargains, volunteer opportunities and advice columns.
Stuff@Night (www.stuffatnight.com) A free offbeat biweekly publication focusing on entertainment events.

ORGANIZED TOURS

BIKE TOURS

Prices include bikes and helmets.
Boston Bike Tours (Map p57; ☎ 617-308-5902; www.bostonbiketours.com; Boston Common; tours $35-40) Offers a full schedule of tours, including Paul Revere's Ride, the Freedom Trail or the Emerald Necklace. Combine your favorite pastimes on the Bike, Beach and Brew Tour, which visits Castle Island, Carson Beach and the Harpoon Brewery.
Urban Adventours (Map p47; ☎ 617-233-7595; www.urbanadventours.com;103 Atlantic Ave; tours $50; 🚇 St Mary's) Founded by avid cyclists who believe the best views of Boston are from a bicycle. The City View Ride provides a great overview of how to get around by bike.

DUCK TOURS

Duck Tours (☎ 617-723-3825; www .bostonducktours.com; adult/child/senior & student $26/17/23; 🕙 9am-dusk Apr-Nov; 🚇 Copley or Science Park) Land and water tours using modified amphibious vehicles from WWII, departing from the Prudential Center and the Museum of Science. Buy tickets in advance.

WALKING TOURS

The granddaddy of walking tours is the Freedom Trail, a 2½-mile trail that traverses the city, from the Boston Common to Charlestown. Most walking tours depart from the Greater Boston Convention & Visitors Bureau information kiosk on the Boston Common, but check the websites for details.

Boston by Foot (☎ 617-367-3766; www .bostonbyfoot.com; tours $8-15) This fantastic nonprofit offers 90-minute walking tours of Boston's neighborhoods. Specialty tours include Literary Landmarks, Boston Underfoot (with highlights from the Big Dig and the T) and Boston for Little Feet – a kid-friendly version of the Freedom Trail.

Boston Movie Tour (☎ 866-668-4345; www.bostonmovietours.net; adult/child/ senior & student $20/10/17) It's not Hollywood, but Boston has hosted its share of famous movie scenes. More than 30 films were shot along Boston's Movie Mile.

Photo Walks (☎ 617-851-2273; www .photowalks.com; adult/youth $25/12; ⏰ 10am & 1pm May-Sep, less often Oct-Apr) A walking tour combined with a photography lesson. Visit Boston's most scenic spots and get some picture-taking tips along the way.

Unofficial Tours (☎ 203-305-9735; www .harv.unofficialtours.com; donations accepted) This unofficial Harvard tour was founded by Harvard alumni who give the inside scoop on history and student life at The University.

TELEPHONE

The US uses a variety of cell-phone systems, most of which are incompatible with the GSM 900/1800 standard used throughout Europe and Asia.

COUNTRY & CITY CODES

The country code for the USA is ☎ 1. All USA phone numbers consist of a three-digit area code followed by a seven-digit local number. Boston's area code is ☎ 617, while surrounding areas may have codes of ☎ 508, ☎ 781 or ☎ 978. Even if you are calling locally in Boston, you must dial ☎ 617 + the seven-digit number. If you are calling long distance, dial ☎ 1 + area code + seven-digit number.

USEFUL PHONE NUMBERS

Emergencies ☎ 911
International Direct Dial Code ☎ 011
Local Directory Inquiries ☎ 411

TIPPING

Many members of the service culture depend on tips to earn a living. Tip taxi drivers (10% to 15%), baggage carriers ($1 per bag) and housekeepers ($3 to $5, more for longer stays). Waiters and bartenders get paid less than minimum wage in the US, so tips constitute their wages. Tip 20% for good service and 15% for adequate service; any less than 15% indicates dissatisfaction with the service.

TOURIST INFORMATION

Boston Common Information Kiosk (Map p57; ☎ 617-426-3115; Tremont & West Sts; ☉ 8:30am-5pm; ⧖ Park St)

Cambridge Visitor Information Kiosk (Map p115; ☎ 617-441-2884, 800-862-5678; www.cambridge-usa.org; Harvard Sq; ☉ 9am-5pm Mon-Sat, 1-5pm Sun; ⧖ Harvard) Detailed information on current Cambridge happenings and self-guided walking tours.

Harvard University Information Center (Map p115; ☎ 617-495-1573; www.harvard .edu; Holyoke Center, 1350 Massachusetts Ave, Cambridge; ⧖ Harvard)

MIT Information Center (off Map p115; ☎ 617-253-4795; http://web.mit.edu /infocenter; Lobby 7, 77 Massachusetts Ave, Cambridge; ☉ 9am-5pm Mon-Fri; ⧖ Central)

National Park Service Visitor Center (NPS; Map p67; ☎ 617-242-5642; www.nps .gov/bost; 15 State St; ☉ 9am-5pm) Plenty of historical literature, a short slide show and free walking tours of the Freedom Trail.

TRAVELERS WITH DISABILITIES

Boston caters to disabled residents and visitors by providing cut curbs, accessible restrooms and ramps on public buildings; but old streets, sidewalks and buildings mean that facilities are not always up to snuff. Accessible sights are noted in the listings with a ⧖ icon. See www.mbta.com/ac-cessibility for information about accessibility on Boston's public transportation.

>INDEX

See also separate subindexes for See (p174), Shop (p175), Eat (p172), Drink (p172) and Play (p174).

000 map pages

000 map pages

☿ DRINK

Bars
Alibi 53
Bukowski Tavern 98
Charlie's Kitchen 120
Corner Pub 87
Cottonwood Café 98
Delux Café & Lounge 106
Fritz 106
Last Hurrah 74
Lower Depths 112
Lucky's 81
Masa 106
Troquet 88

Cafés
Algiers Coffee House 119-20
Caffé Dello Sport 54
Caffe Vittoria 54
Diesel Cafe 120
La Burdick Chocolates 120

Cocktail Lounges
28 Degrees 106
Alibi 53
Drink 81
Flash's Cocktails 106
Minibar 98
Vault 74

Irish Pubs
Burren 120
Farragut House 81
JJ Foley's 73

Microbreweries
Boston Beer Works 53-4

Pubs
21st Amendment 64
Cheers 65
Grendel's Den 120
Intermission Tavern 88

Redbones 120
Silvertone 74
Tavern on the Water 45
Warren Tavern 45

Sports Bars
Bleacher Bar 112
Boston Beer Works 53-4
Caffé Dello Sport 54
Cask 'n Flagon 112
Fritz 106
Johnnie's on the Side 54

🍴 EAT

American
Durgin Park 72
Eastern Standard 110-11
Franklin Café 104
Marliave 73
Paramount 64
Scollay Square 64
Union Bar & Grille 105-6

Asian
Apollo 84-5
Montien 86
My Thai Vegan Café 86
Myers & Chang 104
Suishaya 87
Xinh Xinh 87

Bakeries & Cafés
Café Pamplona 118
Finale Desserterie 85
Flour 80
Other Side Cosmic Café 111
South End Buttery 105
Sportello 80
Zumes Coffee House 45

Burgers
Mr Bartley's Burger Cottage 119
Uburger 111-12

INDEX

000 map pages